COSTUMING A PLAY

COSTUMING A PLAY

INTER-THEATRE ARTS HANDBOOK

BY

ELIZABETH B. GRIMBALL

AND

RHEA WELLS

DESIGNS BY RHEA WELLS

PUBLISHED BY THE CENTURY CO.   ::   New York & London

FOREWORD

The Inter-Theatre Arts Handbook endeavors to give correct and practical information and costume plates as a basis for individual development and artistic variations in the designing and making of costumes. The briefest summary of the history of costumes points out the fact that every kind of costume has come from the tunic, loin cloth and cloak, even the fitted garments are only more complicated developments of these three pieces of wearing apparel.

The designs selected for illustration show the most distinct and characteristic changes in line and silhouette from the early Assyrian and Egyptian to the Civil War period. Each plate also gives designs for the various social castes of the time such as; king, nobleman, middle class, peasant.

The materials and colors in use during each period are described in the separate chapters, where references to books, pictures, sculptures, etc., are also to be found.

There is often a basic pattern for an epoch such as the tunic of the Middle Ages which with slight variations of materials and decorations is correct not only for costumes for that period but for Robin Hood, for a page, a jester, a herald.

Knowledge of this kind helps to simplify the problems of costumes when applied to the stage.

CONTENTS

COSTUMING A PLAY

COSTUMING A PLAY

I

GENERAL INTRODUCTION TO COSTUMING

COSTUME constitutes one of the vital features in the preparation of theatrical performances. It is a very expensive item on the budget, and it is the item which demands most of the drudgery, and taxes the patience and ingenuity of the workers. The success of every period play and pageant depends largely on costumes. They must be planned carefully as to expense, as to correctness historically and symbolically, as to color, line, and decorations. No beautiful results can be obtained by a hit-or-miss method.

It is necessary in the very beginning for the designer to have some knowledge of the general history of costume and of how clothes are inextricably bound up with the progress and development of the race. This knowledge not only enables the designer to be correct as to period but also enlightens him as to the very characteristics of peoples which have induced them to clothe themselves in various ways, and in this way, he is more able to express drama through costume.

The art and designs of every period show the character and requirements of that particular phase of civilization interpreted through dress. In Northern countries, clothes were first worn as a protection to the body against cold weather. This is proved by the fact that skins and furs were the earliest materials used in these climates. In Southern countries, where the climate was moderate and there was little necessity for protection, clothes were first used as decorations. Grass, feathers, pieces of bright colored stones, were used in addition to flowers and leaves. Later on, both the utilitarian and the decorative were combined in costume as may be noted in people of wealth and nobility down to the present time. Leaders of religious orders also adapted this combination in order to distinguish them and their office.

The types of garments for all periods from the most remote down to the present time may be divided into four classifications: The tunic, the loin cloth, the cloak, and fitted garments.

The tunic was the first and simplest form of body covering. It was made of a straight piece of material with an opening cut in the middle, large enough for the garment to pass over the head, and the selvedge sewed together at the sides, leaving a space for the arms to pass through the top. From this simple garment was developed the different types of tunics worn by the Egyptians, the Greeks, the Assyrians, the Romans and many other early nations. Also the waist, shirt, blouse, bodice, smock and all other similar garments which hang from the shoulders.

From the loin cloth, which consisted of a piece of material wrapped around the waist and falling down over the hips and thighs, developed the skirt, apron, trousers, tights, breeches, bloomers and all other garments which hang from the waist.

The cloak, which was an outer garment and used chiefly for protection, developed many different forms; the peplum of the Greeks, the toga and stola of the Romans, the surplice of the church, the cape, shawl, poncho, and other developments of this kind used as outer garments.

4

Aside from these, there is only one important division to be made in the types of garments: the fitted garments. These include the bodice, tights, fitted coat, and all garments which are cut to conform to the contour of the body and differ from the other types in that they do not depend on draperies and folds.

The headdresses which form a very essential part of certain costumes, although they are not garments, must be designed as part of the costume. In the theater, anything that is worn by a character or a group of people having the same characteristics must be considered as part of the costume whether it is a garment, a headdress, jewelry, shoes, gloves, objects which are carried, such as, fans, scepters, wands, or any other accessory which is relative to the character of the person carrying or wearing it. The personality of the character in the drama should be interpreted through the costume as well as the acting. The relation of one character to another and the scenes which two or more characters play together should be taken into consideration by the designer in planning the costumes, as well as line, color and silhouette. This method of planning may be carried out to such a fine degree that one costume will not be complete without the color and design of one or more additional costumes.

The period in which the action is placed must be carefully considered. The characteristics which distinguish one character from the other should be accented and the color scheme which is distinctive of the period must be adhered to. For example, the yellows, reds, yellow greens, turquoise blues, ultramarine blues, black and white of the Egyptians should be the colors used throughout a drama placed in some period of Egyptian history. In addition to an accurate historic knowledge, it is very important for the designer of costumes for dramatic performances to conceive of the individual characteristics of a person as expressed through his clothes. For example, the costume to be designed might be that

5

of an Egyptian princess. It must be Egyptian in line, color and decorations, but it also must express the individual type of that particular princess. Perhaps she was dainty, elusive, or spiritual, or possibly, she was pompous, regal and sensuous.

The designer must remember that his task is to design costumes for a theatrical performance through which a truth, a story or a characteristic is to be shown by the aid of his designs, which must be more than just designs for dress. There are four general types of costumes which are used in theatrical designs: the historical, the fantastic (which includes the symbolical costume), the dance costume, and the modern dress. The designer concerns himself more with line, color and decorations according to accurate historical knowledge when he attempts period costume, and with color and expressive line in connection with fantastic costume. If he is designing dance costume, in addition to line and color, the weight of textiles employed is important. With modern dress, the style is fixed, but the designer must plan the color scheme and the dramatic fitness of each costume to the character as interpreted by the playwright. Certain phases of this interpretation are to be emphasized by costume.

For the theater, it is necessary to exaggerate and over-accent the important points in costume design, because of the artificial lighting and the distance between the audience and the players. In the little theater, this is not carried out to the extent that is necessary in large theaters or in pageantry where a still greater exaggeration is necessary. All unnecessary detail should be eliminated. Single costumes may consist of one or two colors to be effective, and rarely can more than three colors be used to any advantage. The general line of a costume should be accented to the greatest degree possible, and for characters of importance this is absolutely essential in order to give them precedence over minor characters.

In planning designs for costumes, the designer must also consider the materials to be used, the amount required and the construction of the garment. A design to be practical must be something more than an attractive drawing. Unless the effect produced in the drawing can be carried out in the actual garments, the drawing is useless. Therefore, it is necessary for the designer to have some knowledge of cutting and fitting as well as the materials which give the desired effect. He must also understand the relation of the figure to clothes, and how the figure can be helped or hindered by costumes. The comfort of the person wearing the clothes must be considered as well as the beauty of the garment.

Each person who is to be costumed should be carefully measured. The measurements which are to be taken are shown in the diagram. They are as follows: the circumference of the neck and chest, the width of the shoulders, the bust measurement taken with a tape passing well up under the arms, the normal waist line, the hips at the widest part, the distance from the waist to the hip, the distance from the waist over the hip to the edge of the skirt or trousers, the thickness of the thigh, the thickness of the knee, the thickness of the calf, the thickness of the ankle, the arm measurement for the armhole from the point of the shoulder under the armpit, the biceps, the elbow and the wrists, also the length of the sleeve, measuring from the point of the shoulder down the back of the arm to the point where it is to terminate. These measurements are all which are required in any type of garment, and in most garments only the measurements which are necessary need to be taken. In fitting the garments it is important to determine whether or not they are tight in the right places and the fullness is left where it is required. If these points are not accented, the garments do not fit and lose all character unless they depend entirely on draped lines for their character.

In costuming a group which is to present a uniform appearance, certain points or lines such as the length of a skirt or cloak, the position of a waist line and the silhouette, should be considered and emphasized. In making several costumes of the same design, the costume and not the figure of the person who is wearing it should be accented. The measurement for the length of the skirt should be measured from the floor to the edge of the skirt, instead of from the waist line to the edge of the skirt. The same rule applies to measuring cloaks and capes. The waist lines should all be kept as near the same levels as possible. In costumes which require hoopskirts or full sleeves, the fullness or slenderness of the figures should be taken into consideration, so as to correct any noticeable difference between them. Narrow shoulders can be broadened by lengthening the shoulder seams and setting the sleeves farther out. Broad shoulders can be narrowed by shortening the shoulder seams and setting the sleeves in. The hoops which are worn with crinoline dresses should be measured in circumference instead of in proportion to the figure when a number of costumes are to present a similar appearance, such as in the chorus of a musical comedy. Successful and pleasing costuming can be done even by persons who are not specialized designers if they will plan the costumes with regard to emphasizing the vital principles underlying costume design, carefully considering æsthetic, historic and dramatic fitness.

Difference in material for the same design will make the difference, for instance, between the costume of the Puritan and the King, a Cromwell or a James. A correct basis upon which to work would be the mastery of the principles of color and design. A chosen design of the example of a certain period is the simplest thing to carry out if a designer is not very experienced. Such a design must be dramatically good even though very simple. The massing of color, the successful breaking away from the conventional, the effective exaggeration of line, the artist touch, no book on costume can give.

8

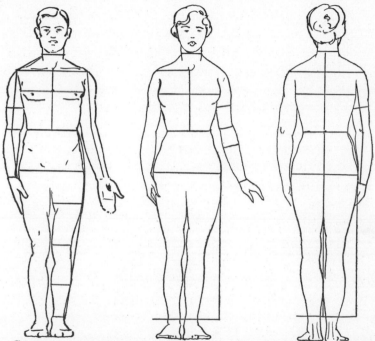

Correct measurements are the first steps in costuming. The description of how to take them is given in Chapter 1.

COLOR

THE color of costumes is one of the two most important factors in a finished production of the visual side of a play. Color must be as carefully considered as any other aspect of costuming. A color scheme is not chosen from the viewpoint of what the individual designer likes or what the individual player fancies is becoming. It must be worked out according to the dramatic requirements of the play, the laws of harmony, the action of certain color in material under certain color used in lighting, and the historic accuracy in regard to the kind of dyes existing at certain periods of the world's history.

The designer must have the knowledge of the simple combinations of color at least. He should know that the combinations of the three primary colors—red, blue and yellow—*in paint or dyes,* make gray or black; and that the combination of the three primary colors—orange, violet and green, or red, blue and green *in light*—make white. He must understand that amber light used alone will gray or kill the value of a scene with blues or greens in it. He must know that a red light will destroy all color except the red values. He must understand that in order to emphasize colors in a stage picture, the color of the light with which he illuminates his scene must be obtained by the use of the three primary colors, as each color will emphasize itself and its variations.

In addition to a knowledge of what colored light will do to color in materials, it is important to consider the use of one color in masses against other colors in masses and how light will affect the appearance of the stage picture. It is also necessary to realize that one color may be used in its various degrees of strength and intensity and give the effect of variety without the use of any other color in a scene. A color scheme in costumes must be planned systematically. The designer should first read the play which is to be presented, noting the colors mentioned in the text, and which colors were used in the period of history during which the action takes place. For example, if the play should be incident of Indian Life, the color would necessarily be influenced by the fact that the Indians in primitive times had only a few vegetable dyes with which to color their dress or themselves, and the color scheme would be confined to these colors. Having noted the limitation of his color chart historically, the designer then plans his color scheme according to what is most suited personally and dramatically to the characters in the play. For a play like "Tantagiles," which has no element of joy or gaiety in the whole action and is built up around the theme which is based on struggle, it would be extremely inappropriate to introduce brilliant light colors. Even rich coloring would not be suitable. A heavy somber treatment would be more effective. That does not mean that all the characters should be costumed in black. Grays, white, purple and neutral shades should be also used. For plays like "Prunella" or "The Wonder Hat," which suggest youth and fantasy, brilliant colors should be used. For a color scheme of this kind, apple green, Nile green, citron, cerise, majenta, mauve, lemon yellow, yellow orange, buff or putty color, or a combination such as black, white, cornflower blue, turquoise blue, jade green, American Beauty red, tangerine and pale yellow would be interesting. These colors all have brilliancy and are light in key without suggesting what is known as pastel shades. For costumes like those of "The Ren-

12

naisance," which were made of heavy damask, brocades and other rich materials, a richer color scheme is required. For these use maroon, rich blues, purples, gold, silver, darker greens, golden brown and bright yellows. In planning costumes for a certain period, always try to discover the colors which predominated at that time. Certain colors at different periods were very popular while others were most unpopular and perhaps not used at all. The best sources of information on any period are the paintings, fabrics and ceramics of that period. These give authentic information as to colors preferred at the time.

The colors for the different characters should be considered in relation to the importance of the characters. An unimportant character should not be costumed in a way that would give it more attention than is due. Neither should a leading character be costumed to subordinate the character. On the other hand, it is possible to overdress the part and subordinate the character and the acting to the clothes.

Scenery is the background against which the actors move and the color of the scenery and the color of the costumes should be planned together by the costume designer and the scenic designer if the same person does not do both. When the costume designer and the scenic designer are the same, this can be carried out much more easily. If blue is used in costume, blue must be used in some of the lights also, even if the scene itself does not require blue lighting. The blue in the costume will in this manner be intensified. Under a white light or an amber light, blue loses its intensity and unless very brilliant takes on a grayish appearance. All warm colors, the reds and the yellows, are brought out by either white or amber light.

13

In plays for children, as much brilliant color as can be used consistently should be employed, as children are particularly attracted by color. Although brilliant colors are used for children's plays, it should not be as crude as color which is required for primitive periods.

If color is used symbolically as, for example, a specific character representing Grief is dressed in gray, then no other gray should be used in the scene. If there is a figure to be dressed in scarlet symbolizing Sin, in order to point this costume no other figure should wear this shade of red. This manner of emphasizing by color is important, and may be done by using a certain color to isolate a figure against a massed group of another color. Suppose there is a massed group costumed in shades of green, one figure or several, if the group is large, may be costumed in gold or black or scarlet to give character to the whole mass.

The designer should have a standard color chart showing color in three dimensions.* The color combinations must be mixed carefully and pure color used as much as possible. Working up and down the chart, the value gradations can be used from light to dark and white to black. Colors become cooler as they descend the scale and warmer as they ascend; colors increase in luminosity or intensity as they become higher or brighter. Yellow has the highest pure intensity and will light up a scene like a flood of sunlight. It is important to remember in connection with a color scheme that dark strong colors must be shown against a light background, and light colors against a dark background. Light color used in backgrounds gives a sense of space and distance, while dark backgrounds often make a stage space seem much smaller than it actually is. In costuming, brilliant colors give brilliancy and movement to a scene while dark colors give strength and dignity.

* Windsor and Newton's Chart, Prang's Color Chart and other standard charts may be used.

14

In order to plan a color scheme, it is absolutely necessary that the person who is doing it should have a correct color sense. Everyone is not so endowed and if a designer, however clever he may be with his line, has not the gift of color, then he had best solicit the assistance of someone who has. Color illuminates the drama emotionally as well as symbolically. A stage set and costumed in tones of cool colors has a distinctly calming effect on an audience, so much so that if a spiritual significance is planned in such a setting, the most successful way to obtain it is to confine the colors to blues, greens, violets and lavenders. On the other hand, a group of dancers costumed in flame and crimson will elicit a round of applause for no other reason than that of the effect of the color itself. It must be remembered in dealing with color, that black and white are not colors but only values. There is too much white used in most big spectacles. It is a great mistake and a very common one to costume great groups of Greek maidens or Roman youths in white. The designer who does this has not looked up his period. Black is exceedingly depressing but tremendously effective if used sparingly. Grays and purples have the same emotional value as black and are much more interesting under light. A designer of costumes cannot make too careful a study of the science of color and color combinations.

III

DYEING AND DECORATING TEXTILES

AS color is one of the vital elements which make for value and beauty in stage costumes and draperies, art directors would find it of great assistance in their work to understand methods of coloring and decorating textiles.

Dyeing is probably the most popular way of obtaining interesting color effects through the medium of textiles, and a method which can be recommended as both economical and extremely decorative. One of the properties of color under light is its remarkable ability to give a variety of rich effects to the most ordinary material. A piece of heavy, unbleached muslin dyed first in a red and blue mixture of cotton dye, then redipped in a royal basic purple dye will take on the appearance of a brocaded velvet robe when made into a costume and lighted with the three primary light colors. A piece of cheap sateen dipped unevenly into a bath of chrysoidine (a deep orange basic dye), when rough dried and subjected to the proper lighting, has the quality of panne velvet.

It is never necessary to use very expensive materials for costumes and hangings but it is necessary to give the illusion of richness when required. This effect generally depends upon the brilliancy of color and the apparent weight of textiles used. Materials must first be selected from the point of view of textiles and then colored to get the desired brilliancy. This is done by dyeing them unevenly in whatever color the general plan requires. There are several kinds of dye stuffs, but three of these will serve the purpose for theater dyeing. They are: The Cotton or Salt Dyes, chemically right for dyeing linen or any other vegetable goods, so called because it is necessary to use a little salt in order to set the colors; the Silk or Acid Dyes, chemically right for dyeing silks, wools or other animal textiles, and the Basic Dyes, very strong analine dye stuffs, with a powerful affinity for acids and which give a peculiar brilliancy when used. This class of dye stuffs is extremely fugitive to sunlight and it is a risk to use them for coloring costumes to be shown in out-of-door pageants, although the intensity of the color will last for one or two performances. If the production is to be given under artificial light, the basic dyes are very valuable because of the vibrant quality resulting from this method of coloring. These dyes may be used on silk, wool, straw or feathers or leather directly, but cotton has no affinity for them unless first dipped in a mild solution of cotton dyes of the color required for the foundation.

Flat even dyeing is not interesting for theatrical effects. It is better to endeavor to obtain graded effects. If a blue curtain is wanted, the most beautiful result can be obtained by first dipping the material in a bath of pale blue cotton dye, and then redipping in one of the basic blues—Imperial, Methylene or Victoria. When light is played on such a curtain, there is a vibrant sparkling beauty which entirely does away with a feeling of an ordinary curtain of a flat color. All dyeing of costumes to be worn under artificial light on the stage should be done in this way. For instance, a better purple results from first dipping the material in blue and topping it with red, than from a bath of purple dye already mixed. The effect is vivid and living in one case and quite dead and monotonous in the other.

18

It is not necessary for the experimenter in dyes to stock up with all the dye stuffs on the market. He should have several pounds of the primary cotton colors and supplement this with the following list of basic dyes: Victoria blue, Methylene blue, Imperial blue, Victoria green, Auramine yellow, Chrysoidine gold, Rhodammine red and Safranine red. These can be bought at either of the large dye manufacturers, such as DuPont DeNemours and the National Aniline and Chemical Company.

There is no hard and fast rule about the amount of water and dye stuff to be used. This will depend a good deal on the effects desired. The best way to learn is to experiment a little and use individual taste and judgment. There are definite directions, however, about mixing dyes, which the beginner must know. All cotton and silk dyes must be dissolved in warm water before being poured into the dye bath, and to the bath of the silk dye should be added a small amount, say half a teaspoonful, of acetic acid. If the result of dyeing in silk dye is unsatisfactory, the dye can be boiled out of the material in soapsuds made of "Silk Soap" or some other equally oily soap. The color can then be run back into the material by adding a little acetic acid. The basic dyes must be dissolved in a little acetic acid before being used in hot water for the dye bath. Once basic dye is set, there is no way to get it out of material except by fading it in the sun. To dye feathers or straw, basic dye must be first dissolved in oxalic acid. All dye stuff must be dissolved in a small quantity of hot water before being poured into the larger dye bath. Cotton goods must be boiled in their dye in order to get any depth of color and to make them fast. All materials should be thoroughly rinsed before dyeing and after dyeing before they are hung up to dry. It is best to dry dye fabrics in the shade, and if basic dyes are used, indoors.

There are several very interesting ways to vary the results in dyeing. The simplest of these is graduating the color so that some portion of the material is darker than another. This is done by holding the material so that when it is dipped, one portion of the material gets an additional layer of the dye while one portion gets possibly only one dipping. The secret of getting an evenly graduated color is the constant dipping of the material in clear water between the times it is redipped in the dye. The method known as "Tied and Dyed" is more complicated and very decorative. Material may be tied across the breadths at regular intervals or in circles after having been first dipped into one color and then dyed with another color. For instance, suppose a scarf is dyed first in light yellow, then the ends of the scarf are tied in loops. The center of the scarf may be taken up and tied three times with a tape. The material is then redipped, first, in Methylene blue for the ends of the scarf and Chrysoidine and Rhodammine for the middle of the scarf. When the material is taken out of the dye and thoroughly rinsed in order to get rid of the loose dye which may rub off when dry, the scarf is untied with the result that there is a decorative, light gold border in the peacock green ends and there is a gold circle in the flame-colored center of the scarf. For rainbow dyeing, the material may be held without tieing it and dipped from one primary color to the other with the result, when finished, that a scarf will have all the colors of the rainbow, both primary and complementary. A definite design in tie dyeing may be obtained by outlining the design with a needle and coarse thread.

The commercial dyes on the market are very good and prepared for use with explicit directions as to quantity and method of mixing, but if large amounts of dye stuffs are to be used it is more economical to buy by the pound from the manufacturers. The best reference book on dyes and their use is "Dyes and Dyeing," by Charles E. Pellew.

The other method of decorating textiles is known as the direct application of colors. This means painting the material instead of dyeing. A very interesting effect can be obtained by painting unbleached muslin with a thin solution of dry color mixed with water and sized with liquid glue. The result of such a method is exceedingly beautiful under artificial light. A very ordinary material such as unbleached muslin looks like soft velvet after being painted. Dry color can be bought by the pound from any paint store, also powdered glue. The paint is mixed with water according to the amount needed to make a thin solution. Into this is poured a little liquid glue. The color is then applied to the material with a broad, flat brush so that the material is painted all over its surface. This method of coloring textiles is very quick and much less trouble than dyeing and gives an interesting variety.

Paint is also applied to material in designs. Free hand or stencil. The latter method is the best to use unless the decorator is a trained draughtsman and understands thoroughly the proportion of design. A stencil is made in the following manner: A design is drawn on a piece of white paper and filled in with India Ink. This is then placed underneath stencil paper which is a specially prepared translucent paper known as "stencil paper." The pattern shows through the translucent paper and can be drawn with a sharp pencil. The design is then cut out with a sharp knife known as a "stencil knife." The stencil design is now ready to be used over and over again by placing it on the material to be decorated and painting in whatever colors are desired, through the open places. In case the person who is painting the stencils does not understand how to draw design, standard designs already cut and ready for use can be bought at any art supply shop. People who are painting stencils should be careful to obtain for themselves the proper brush with which to make their design. The stencil knife is also important and the best for any use are the Japanese Knives.

The care of stencils is very important. They should be used on one side and carefully cleaned off after each using. Stenciling is very effective when a bold design is needed and a design which must stand out giving the effect of brocade or appliqué. This method of decorating is particularly effective in spectacular performances.

IV

LIGHTING COSTUMES

STAGE lighting has several functions in its application to the production of a play. It illuminates the scene, it gives a certain emotional atmosphere to the drama, it tells the time of day, the season of the year and it emphasizes the color in settings and costumes.

In order to bring out the color of costumes as planned, it is necessary to include in the lighting scheme the colors which will emphasize the color scheme of the costumes. This must be done without changing the value of the light which lights the scene itself. It can be done if the footlights and overhead borders carry the three primary colors, red, yellow and blue, or orange, violet and green. The result of this use of light will be a natural light which if properly focused will not confuse the general lighting which is planned from correct sources, but will bring out each costume in its proper color value. For instance, a scene may be lighted from a window through which is introduced a flood of amber light to give the effect of sunlight. If the costumes of the players happen to be complementary colors of amber and red, the amber flood will accentuate and enhance the colors. But if the costumes should be blues, greens or violets, the entire value of their colors will be lost under the amber flood, unless somewhere there is introduced some blue or green light. This is usually done by using some footlights simply to give color or overhead lights used directly inside the proscenium frame.

If, on the other hand, the scene is lighted from within by table lamps or wall brackets, so that the predominant light will be the rose of interior illumination, it is equally necessary to use blue somewhere in the scheme in order to preserve the color of blue costumes. By the use of baby spot lights from the footlights, or from the wings, certain costumes can be still more emphasized by flooding them with their own color.

When a scene is largely lighted by pale green usually employed to simulate moonlight, the costumes should be carefully planned from colors which will not be dulled or too much changed by the green light. Blues, violets, yellows, turkey red, may be safely used. Turkey red is such a brilliant color that it will keep its value and intensity under almost any lighting. Blues are very easily affected and become gray under amber, or if there is sufficient yellow in them, they will become a greenish yellow. Violets are easily affected and are completely destroyed by an amber light, becoming an ugly brown. When a costume is made of materials which combine several colors blended in the way a gray is obtained by using the three primary colors one on top of the other, it becomes exceedingly beautiful under light combining the three primary colors, because each color brings out its own color. If a costume is colored by dyeing with graduated dyes, so that peacock green, for instance, is more blue at one end of the garment and more green at the other, it is necessary to light such a costume with two colored lights.

The usual equipment of a modern theater supplies all that is necessary to light scenes and give color to draperies. Footlights and overhead borders are usually supplied in blue, amber and white. The best theaters have borders of small spot lamps in addition to the ordinary bulb. This enables light to be focused and angled in different directions. The color of light is obtained by using gelatine in metal frames which fit in front of the lens lights, which is a technical name for spot lights. All colors can be obtained in gelatine which comes in large pieces and costs from 20 to 60 cents a sheet. In addition to footlights and borders, what is known as the portable equipment is used. This consists of open-box flood lights on stands, spot or lens lights on stands placed wherever it is desired to introduce extra lights. It is very important that all colored material for costumes be tested under the colored lights planned for a scene before actually making them up. It is impossible for the best designer to imagine accurately just how his color scheme is going to visualize until he sees it under light. The color will vary in value and intensity according to the degree of light used, the angle of the lamp and the number of lamps used in a scene. It is suggested that all colored materials for costumes be tried for effect under flood lights through the medium of every color in a spectrum. In this way, the mistakes and disappointments will be avoided.

V

MATERIALS

THE kind of materials used in the making of costumes for the stage is a vital factor in the appearance of the finished costume. The weave, the weight, and the surface of the cloth must be taken into consideration when a design is ready to be executed, in order that the costumes may express the period of the play, the social class and the dramatic situation of the character presented.

Climatic conditions influenced to a great extent the kinds of material used; for instance, races living in warm latitudes used cotton and linen and other thin tissues, while those inhabiting cold climates used wool or heavier weaves of cotton and linen. The next condition which influenced the kind of materials used was that of social distinction with wealth. The rich and powerful of all ages and nations had more elaborate raiment than the poor and lowly.

In costuming for the theater, it is not necessary to use the actual material worn in the period, but it is necessary to give the effect of the correct material.

For this purpose we must consider materials under the three heads of weave, weight, and surface. Poor people and peasants wore coarsely woven cloth. Royalty and powerful persons made their robes of rich, heavy material.

Certain materials such as silk and velvet were not known to very early or primitive races. Certain materials were absolutely expressive of certain races. All these points must be taken into consideration when a play or a pageant is costumed.

Under the heading of Weave, we divide the materials according as they are coarse or fine. Coarse material includes such textiles as: Tarlatan, mosquito netting, fish net, toweling, straw matting, burlap, coarse muslin or coarse marquisette and any coarse weave of any material.

Fine material includes such textiles as: Chiffon, georgette, mull, gauzes of all kinds, cheesecloth, crêpe de chine, voile, lawn, challis, etc.

This particular division of the weave of a cloth is also subdivided into another division according to whether a material is soft and clinging or stiff. Buckram and crinoline are of a coarse weave and very stiff. Chiffon and mull are fine and very soft, but metal cloths of all kinds may be either coarse or fine but are always more or less stiff.

Under the heading of Weight, materials are divided according as they are light or heavy.

The heavy textiles are such as: Velvet, plush, denim, some kinds of silk crêpe, some satins, corduroy, flannel, some grades of unbleached muslin, turkish toweling, felt, jersey, cotton, flannel, ratine, etc.

Under the division of light materials some of the textiles are: Silk crêpe, crêpe de chine, China silk, georgette, chiffon, mull, tulle, tarlatan, nets of all kinds, laces, gauzes of all kinds, cheesecloth, voile, challis, muslin lawn, etc.

Under the heading of Surface, textiles are divided according as they are dull or shining—that is, have luster.

Textiles having luster are: Metallic cloths, such as gold cloth, metallic oilcloth, which comes in many colors, silver cloth, bronze cloth, pineapple cloth in any color, cloth which has been gilded, silvered or bronzed, heavy satins, taffeta, sateens, China silk, silk damask (which is also a heavy material), argentine, poplin, silk net, glazed silk.

Textiles having dull surfaces are: Velvet, silk crêpe, duyveteen, corduroy, unbleached muslin, flannel, cotton flannel or crêpe, ratine, turkish toweling, cotton net and tarlatan, leather, cotton damask, cretonne, etc.

Materials should also be considered, aside from the three main divisions already described, according to whether the surface is plain, figured or striped. This point is important because in certain periods and with certain races, the woven decorations of fabrics were very typical and expressive of their characteristic taste in color and decoration. Stripes are characteristic of the Arab, the Egyptian, the Roman, while diagonals are typical of the Assyrian. Flowered materials were much in vogue in certain centuries, particularly the 18th and early 19th, also flowered brocades were much used in the days of Queen Elizabeth.

If the designer is careful to consider materials from the viewpoint of simulating the weave and weight and surface of the textiles of the particular period which he is costuming, he will make designs and costumes which are both beautiful and correct.

VI

COSTUMING A PAGEANT

COSTUMING a pageant is a problem all its own and in considering this problem there are three aspects. A pageant may be given indoors. It may be given out of doors, either at night under artificial lights or in the day under strong sunlight. The time and the conditions of light will influence the color and to a lesser degree the line of the costumes.

In pageantry the color should be intensified and the massing of color increased as much as possible. The color and shape of the costume is of much greater importance than the texture or any amount of detail which may be added. Costumes which consist of one or two colors are more effective than those which are made of expensive materials with many elaborate details. At a distance, the detail is lost and two or three colors in textile design, unless it is very bold in color and design, are likely to be lost. A bold stencil design on dyed muslin of the right color is more effective in most instances than a very costly brocade, and at a distance will have the effect of a brocade.

A pageant by its nature is a spectacle and is made up of massed groups rather than individual units. It is played in large auditoriums, the largest theater or out of doors where the audience is comparatively far away from the performers. Costume, therefore, must be regarded according to the viewpoint of what will carry to an audience at a distance. Line is the first point. All line must be correct, but it must be exaggerated and the silhouette must be emphasized. Detail of decoration is unnecessary but form and color are most vital. Simplicity is the most powerful way of giving variety to costuming in pageantry. The problem of giving unity and yet variety to large groups of people, costumed in the same period, presents itself as a grave difficulty on account of the danger of the scene becoming monotonous in value and color. This must be carefully considered. Take, for example, a group of Orientals in the market place of ancient Samaria at the time of the Assyrian domination. The colors used in those days were limited to the primitive blues, reds and yellows, crudely brilliant with little variation. The line of the garment was universally flowing as to under-robe, over-robe and headdress. A large group can be made uninteresting and monotonous if the designer is not watchful. It will not do to give too much individual variety. If this is done, the value of masses is immediately lost. It is possible, however, to keep unity by carrying a basic color scheme through the entire mass, varying the decoration and the color of headdresses. The monotony of line may be broken by making a difference in the manner of draping the mantles and veils of the women and the turbans of the men.

It is valuable in costuming masses where the color scheme is not limited by historical differences to use one color in different tones throughout a group. This is especially true of symbolical pageants. Again it is often tremendously impressive to costume a great mass of people in one or two colors carrying the same type or line throughout.

In planning outstanding figures, especially of symbolical characters, the designer can scarcely over-emphasize line or color, particularly if the spectacle is given out of doors where space is so immense as compared with the human figure.

The color scheme for a pageant must be planned very differently according to whether the performance is to be indoors or out of doors at night or out of doors in the day. Under artificial light a color scheme can be more subtle and varied depending on the color of the lighting effects. This is true whether indoors or out of doors. If the pageant is produced out of doors in the day, the color scheme must be planned with regard to the fact that the costumes will be shown against a green background. Greens and blues must necessarily be sparingly used, and if used at all, shades should be selected which are either much darker or much lighter than the green of the grass and the trees. No pastel shades such as are used under artificial light will carry at a distance out of doors in the sunlight. Pale blue, pale pink, pale green, orchid or any delicate tint of this kind will look almost white and quite without character under strong daylight. The effect of a pastel group may be obtained by using quite strong tones of these colors. The best effects in outdoor pageantry by daylight are obtained by using very strong, crude colors.

In selecting materials for pageant costumes it is important to remember that heavier, coarser materials may be used with much more effect at a distance. Decorations should be simply and boldly executed. Delicate lines and shadings are completely lost as well as intricate details of jewelry or laces. The important point, therefore, to remember in costuming a pageant is that the costumes must have the most careful planning and designing as well as execution, because upon the costumes, especially in an out-of-door pageant, depends the entire verity of the drama, historically and æsthetically.

33

EGYPTIAN COSTUME

The garments used in Egyptian costume were very simple in construction. They were (1) the Tunic, (2) the Loin Cloth, (3) the Skirt. The tunic was a tight-fitting garment usually with short sleeves reaching half way to the elbows and decorated with a band of alternating stripes of two or three colors about three inches deep. This was not a long garment but usually reached just below the hips, except in some instances such as in the costume of a priest or scribe where it was lengthened almost to the ankles. This garment was worn by both men and women.

Loin cloths which were worn by the men were made of straight pieces of material fastened round the waist by a band or belt about two inches in width, or for slaves' costumes by a cord which may be made of a piece of material twisted or rolled and tied in a double knot or bowknot. These loin cloths had many variations. The lower corners may have been rounded, square, or the overlapping end may have been cut diagonally. In some instances where the lower corners were rounded and the cloth was only long enough to overlap six or eight inches in front a straight piece of material hung down in front about three or four inches below the curved edges of the loin cloth. Slaves costumes very often included no other form of apparel. This garment was worn by all classes and at all periods.

The skirt which was worn by the women usually came up to the breast and was supported by two straps about two inches in width, which were fastened to the skirt in front just below the breast, carried over the shoulders, and again attached to the skirt in the middle of the back. This skirt resembles very much in appearance the princesse type of dress which is fitted to the body as far down as the widest part of the hips and cut straight from there to the bottom. Some of these skirts are elaborately decorated with painted or woven patterns or designs, the favorite motif being arrangements of stripes.

Wide collars were worn by both men and women of the nobility and gods and goddesses. They were circular bands which fitted over the shoulders and lay flat like a yoke and were six to eight inches in width. Some of them were made entirely of rows of beads, of gold and different colored stones, while others were woven materials with a design painted on them. Wristlets, armlets and anklets were also worn extensively with elaborate costumes by people of the nobility and upper classes. The armlets were worn over the biceps. These pieces of ornament were usually three to four inches in width and for a single costume were all decorated with the same design and colors.

Priests' costumes usually consisted of a long white skirt reaching from the waist to the ankles and secured by a girdle or broad band of white material which was spread out in the back and fastened in front by overlapping and drawing one end under and over the other, permitting the ends to hang down in front. All the fullness of the skirt should be drawn to the front in order to make folds. With this was worn a tunic which fitted the body closely and had a short sleeve for the left arm and cut out with only an armhole on the right side. Over this was worn a leopard skin with the head and fore-legs drawn over the right shoulder and fastened to the tunic in front, the other part of the skin passing diagonally across the back and fastened over the left hip at the waist. Priests usually went without wigs, showing their bald or shaved heads, which were common among the Egyptians, and which accounts for the elaborate wigs and headdresses which were worn so extensively.

36

Chief among the headdresses are the crowns of upper and lower Egypt, which are shown in the illustrations. A ruler of both wore a crown with a combination of the two. The fillet which was a straight band or ribbon about an inch wide was worn by women, and tied in a bowknot at the back of the head. The asp which ornamented the front of so many headdresses, including the fillet, was a sign of nobility.

The materials which were used by the Egyptians were cotton, linen and wool. Sandals were worn by the upper classes and were made by fastening thongs which were drawn over the instep and fastened to the soles on either side of the foot. The soles were pointed and turned up two or three inches front and back. The Egyptians used green, blue and red, a combination which was particularly favored at all times and in all parts of the country. At times black and yellow were added. White was also used very extensively. The reds were vermilion, terra cotta, Indian, Venetian and all the reds toward orange. Red such as rose, majenta, madder and the other reds bordering on purple were not used. The greens were yellow-green, and the blues which were used were turquoise and blue-green and ultramarine. A great many costumes were entirely black and white.

REFERENCES FOR VERIFICATION AND VARIATIONS

Wilkinson, "Ancient Egyptians"
Racinet, "Le Costume Historique"
Hottenroth, "Le Costume"

Metropolitan Museum Catalogue of Egyptian Collections
Paintings on old walls and tombs

SOME PLAYS AND CHARACTERS FOR WHICH THESE COSTUMES ARE APPROPRIATE

All Plays of Ancient Egypt
Story of Moses' early life
Anthony and Cleopatra

Osiris
Isis
Some plays of Dunsany's

PLATE I

No. 1 shows the figure of a man wearing a striped headdress which is made of a piece of material drawn straight across the forehead and fastened at the back of the head. Two long tabs fall down the front of the shoulders and the rest of the material hangs down the back. He wears a loin cloth of striped material and a tight-fitting tunic, or in some instances the tunic may be omitted, and the costume completed with the wide collar, striped armlets, wristlets and anklets.

No. 2 shows the figure of a priest with shaved head wearing a tunic with one sleeve of semi-transparent material. He also wears a long skirt with the fullness drawn round to the front and a wide sash, wrapped round the waist and tied in front with the ends hanging down and edged with a fringe. Over the right shoulder is drawn the head and forelegs of a leopard skin which is secured in that position and drawn diagonally across the back and again fastened on the left hip. This costume is made entirely of white material, semi-transparent, with the exception of the tiger skin.

No. 3 shows a scribe with bald head, wearing a short cape over his left shoulder and a long skirt which is drawn up and fastened in front. Over this is a wide girdle around the waist which is tied in front. The ends are fringed and hang down half way between the knees and the ankles. The cape may be made of heavy bleached muslin. It is fastened under the right arm by tying two strings which are attached to the corners. The skirt and sash should be made of sheer white lawn.

No. 4 shows a king wearing a short black beard attached to the strap which passes under his chin. Over his shoulders he wears the wide collar used by both men and women, which was usually made of six alternating rows of long beads separated by rows of smaller round beads. He is wearing a short skirt supported by straps and reaching just below the waist line. Over this is placed the loin cloth, which is of plain material either white or yellow, and around his waist he wears a wide girdle of striped material. The wristlets, armlets and anklets which always match each other are also striped. On his feet he is wearing a pair of straw sandals turned up at the toe and heel and fastened by thorns. This costume should be made of muslin of a heavy quality and striped ticking showing red, yellow and blue or black stripes. The headdress should be made of buckram painted either orange or gold.

Fig. 1   Fig. 2   Fig. 3   Fig. 4

Figures 1 and 4 represent respectively a nobleman and a king; the headdress being the most important difference. The costumes of figures 2 and 3 vary slightly and yet these variations mark the difference between a priest and a scribe. A slave wears only a loin cloth and a headdress folded like the one for figure 1.

WIGS

No. 1. Skull cap which was worn extensively by Egyptians in the absence of the wig. This is particularly effective with costumes which consist simply of a loin cloth or plain tunic and loin cloth. To make one of these skull caps the easiest method is to take the crown of a white felt hat, wet it, draw down snugly over the skull and outline the edges where it is to be cut with a pencil, then trim off all material not needed. The same method may be applied in making other types of headdresses which fit closely, such as helmets, etc.

Fig. 1   Fig. 2   Fig. 3   Fig. 4   Fig. 5

Nos. 2, 3, 4 and 5 show different types of wigs which were worn by the Egyptians and are drawn in profile. These wigs may be made of worsted fastened to a tight cap, or hemp rope raveled out and dyed black. In No. 5 the space between the front lock and the back is where the hair is divided by the shoulder.

HEADDRESSES

No. 1 shows the headdress of a queen ornamented in front with the asp, which was a sign of nobility. The asp on the headdress is wearing the crown of upper and lower Egypt. At the back is the hawk with spread wings.

Nos. 2 and 3 are the crowns of upper and lower Egypt.

No. 3 shows the king's headdress which may be worn with costume No. 4 in Plate 1. No. 5 shows the hawk which was used as headdress. Headdresses should be shaped out of buckram and a pattern should be cut first of heavy wrapping paper and fitted to the persons who are to wear them. After the shape has been made the color can be painted on or gilded, as required, to carry out the design. If temper color is used care must be taken not to wet the buckram too much as this will soften it and cause it to lose its shape.

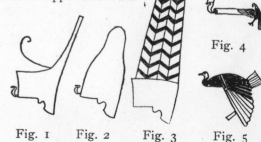

Fig. 1   Fig. 2   Fig. 3   Fig. 4   Fig. 5

40

The illustration shows a tunic with short sleeves. This was made from a straight piece of material, with seams up the sides as far as the armpits, and an opening which fastened in front and was just large enough for the head to pass through. The Egyptians for the most part wore short tunics which were very close fitting in the body, as indicated by their paintings and sculptures.

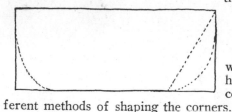

LOIN CLOTH

This shows a rectangular piece of material which was wound round the waist and reached half way down between the hips and the knees, covering the thighs. Dotted lines indicate different methods of shaping the corners.

LOIN CLOTHS

No. 1 shows a straight loin cloth wrapped round the waist and secured by a cord tied in a bowknot. No. 2 shows the same kind of loin cloth with rounded corners secured at the waist by a band of material tied in a double knot. No. 3 shows a pair of short trousers similar to the ones worn at the present time in athletics. No. 4 shows a loin cloth with corners cut diagonally and a tab hanging down in front underneath the loin cloth.

Fig. 1   Fig. 2   Fig. 3   Fig. 4

41

PLATE II

No. 1. Figure wearing costume of plain material consisting of a skirt fitted from the bust to the hips and supported by wide straps over the shoulders. This is also the pattern for No. 3 and No. 4, the only difference being in the width of the straps.

No. 2. This costume consists of a cape which fastens in front and is cut away at the bottom, a tunic cut in a V front and back, and a skirt which is wrapped around the waist and fastened with a cord. The necklace is painted on a circular piece of material.

No. 3. This shows a figure wearing a striped headdress and a garment which is simply a skirt supported by two bands of beads which are fastened in front below the breast, pass over the shoulders and again are attached to the skirt in the center of the back. The skirt is covered with a scale design, which should be stenciled on in four colors which repeat in the order given, red, dark green, turquoise blue, yellow, ocher, red, etc. Detailed design may be seen in the detailed drawing at the left of figure. From the knees down the design of the skirt is of alternating stripes of dark yellow-green and yellow ocher. The wristlets and anklets are made of bead work similar to that used for the straps. Under the collar and skirt is worn a short tight-fitting sleeveless tunic.

No. 4. This figure shows the costume of a queen of Egypt. She wears a headdress after the conventionalized design of the hawk. Her dress is of sheer linen; a fine quality of lawn is a good substitute. The design is carried out in terra cotta, blue and green. It follows the conventional wings of the hawk below the knees, and the stripes used are both broad and narrow. Her dress is made like the dress of Figure 3. Her jewels can be made of dyed or painted wooden beads, china beads and varnished sealing-wax applied on heavy buckram.

Fig. 1   Fig. 2   Fig. 3   Fig. 4

Figure 1 is the dress worn by a slave. Figure 3 is the costume worn by the low class women of Egypt. Figure 2 is the middle class woman, while figure 4 is a woman of the court. The same style more elaborate and with the royal headdress becomes the garb of a queen or goddess.

ASSYRIAN COSTUME

There were three parts to the Assyrian garments: (1) the tunic or shirt; (2) the skirt; (3) the cloak or cape. In addition to these, belts or girdles eight or ten inches in width and highly ornamented with characteristic designs, were part of the men's costumes. Most of the clothes which were worn by the Assyrians were ornamented and the costumes of the kings and queens, officials and eunuchs who attended the kings were extremely elaborate. Some of them were entirely covered with designs. Jewelry, fringes and tassels were used to a great extent, and border designs seem to have been very popular with these people.

Judging by the figures which are shown in ancient Assyrian sculptures most of the materials used for costumes were heavy and probably woven of wool. Some authorities mention silk in describing ancient Assyrian costumes, but it seems doubtful as there is nothing in the painting or sculpture which would indicate material of this texture having been used. Silk was not known among the Egyptians and Greeks of that period and it is hardly probable that it was employed by the Assyrians.

The coloring was richer and more varied than that of the Egyptians. The Assyrians used a variety of purples, maroons, light yellows, oranges, blues, blacks, ochers and greens. This coloring combined with gold jewelry and ornaments and embellished with many colored stones produced an exceedingly rich effect. Both long and short tunics were worn by the men; the long tunic reached to the ankles, while

45

the short tunic, which was usually edged with a fringe and narrow border design, barely reached the knees, including the fringe. In many instances half skirts or aprons are shown worn by the men, which were secured by a cord around the waist and were of varying length between the knee and the ankle and banded with fringe down the sides and across the bottom. A circular strip of material about forty inches long, bearing a border design with a fringe along one side, was often worn by the men. It was put on over the head and the right arm and worn diagonally across the front and back, passing over the left shoulder and under the right arm. This was put on over all the garments with which it was worn. The tunic worn by Assyrian men was a sort of tight-fitting shirt with short sleeves and round neck edged with a narrow border about an inch wide. A great amount of jewelry was worn by the men. Rings, earrings, bracelets and armlets were invariably worn by men of high rank.

Sandals with straight soles and heel pieces were worn. Shoes of yellow leather which came half way up to the knees and were laced up the front were used. These were worn by soldiers over a covering for the leg, which appears to be a sort of stocking made of chain armor with a fastening around the leg just below the knee. The hair of both men and women was held back by a band passing over the forehead and tied at the back of the head. All men are shown with full beards and long hair.

The women wore an inner shirt and an outer tunic which fell to the feet and was bordered with a fringe. Over this they wore a cloak which resembled a cape and which was fringed all the way around the lower edge. This cloak was worn over the right shoulder drawn across the back under the left armpit and once around the body and was secured by drawing it tight. The corners were rounded and the end which passed over the right shoulder hung down only as far as the elbow. Slave women were costumed only in a tunic with a cord tied around the waist. More elaborate dresses were ornamented with border designs and patterned all over with medallions, squares or circles. Old Testament stories should be costumed in this manner. This dress seems to have been common to all regions of the lower part of the Euphrates and the Tigris.

The materials which will produce a good effect in these costumes are unbleached muslin, duck, cotton flannel dyed and decorated with stenciled designs. Draping the material is not required in the making of these garments as they are all cut to hang straight or are slightly fitted.

REFERENCES FOR VERIFICATION AND VARIATION

Layard, "Monuments of Nineveh"   Hottenroth, "Le Costume"
Racinet, "Le Costume Historique"   Planchet, "Cyclopedia of Costumes"
  Assyrian Sculptures—Slabs carved in bas-relief with great minuteness of detail.

SOME PLAYS AND CHARACTERS FOR WHICH ASSYRIAN COSTUMES ARE APPROPRIATE

Assyrian Gods and Goddesses

Ashtoreth or Ishtar

Baal, etc.

Plays Based on Old Testament Stories:
  Judith and Holofernes
  Solomon
  Moses
  David
  Job
  The Maccabees
  The Prophets and Kings of Israel, etc.

PLATE III

No. 1 shows the dress of a soldier wearing a short-sleeved tunic decorated with bands of simple design, a short skirt which reaches almost to the knees, over which, across the back, is worn a short apron-like garment edged with a fringe. At the side there is a long tab hanging down, one edge of which is also fringed. The legs are covered with a chequered or plaid material fastened with a band just below the knees. The lower end of this leg covering is confined by the top of high shoes made of yellow or green leather and laced up in front. The hair is held back by a fillet. Around the waist is worn a wide girdle.

No. 2 shows the costume of a priest wearing a straight tunic with one sleeve on the right side. On his head he wore a dome-shaped helmet with a spike on top. Around his waist he wore a wide girdle ornamented with a bordered design, which is repeated on the edge of the tunic and on the pointed tab which hangs down the right side below the edge of the tunic and is edged on one side with a fringe.

No. 3 shows a type of dress which was worn by slaves and captives. It consisted of a tunic with short sleeves and a wide girdle and a fillet for the hair.

No. 4 shows a king's costume.

Early portraits of kings show them in thick quilted skirts to the ankles and quilted turbans. The skirts were sometimes narrower as in Figure 4 and heavily decorated in squares or circles. A king wore gold armlets, necklets, crown and anklets. He often carried a small parasol as a sign of rank. Sandals or leather boots were worn as Assyria had a rigorous climate.

Fig. 1   Fig. 2   Fig. 3   Fig. 4

The simple tunic almost to the knee and the wide girdle are carried through all the social grades of the Assyrians. Figure 1 is a slave without decoration of any kind. Fringe and border decorations were used extensively, not only by kings, as in figure 4, where the length of the skirt and the diadem denote his rank, but in the priest of figure 2 and the soldier of figure 3.

49

PLATE IV

No. 1. This figure shows the straight tunic worn by the lower class of Assyrian women. It is also used as an under-tunic for the better classes. It is decorated with a simple design of open and solid squares used as a border around the bottom of the skirt, the arm-holes and the neck. This woman wears no sandals, her hair is confined by a simple band.

No. 2. This figure shows the over mantle which is worn with the tunic just described. It is decorated with square design and fringe. The manner of wearing this mantle is described in the text of the chapter on Assyrian costume.

No. 3. This figure shows the costume of the women of the upper classes. Her under tunic is covered with circle designs. Her mantle is decorated with a border of squares and is fringed. Her headdress is a gold band ornamented with jewels, if the wearer is a queen, and with simpler decorations if she is of lesser rank. These tunics were usually made of wool. In order to give the effect of wool, the substitute must be soft and of a close weave. The decorative borders must be stenciled on a soft quality of unbleached muslin, a good material for the tunics. All jewels should be heavy and barbaric in design. Stone was rare in Assyria and Babylonia. For this reason even pebbles were valued for decorative purposes.

Fig. 1   Fig. 2   Fig. 3

The costumes of the Assyrian women varied little except in border decoration and fringes.   Figure 1 is the simple under tunic, figure 2 a woman
of the lower class and figure 3 a queen or woman of the upper classes.

51

GREEK COSTUME

The Greek costume consists essentially of two parts: first, the tunic; second, the cloak or peplum. The tunic which was worn by the Greeks, both men and women, had many variations which were achieved by variety of draping. They have been long or short, pleated or plain, of figured or solid color materials. The women often wore one tunic over another, which is called a super-tunic, the outer garment being draped in such a manner as to show the undergarment falling down over the shoulders and the upper arm in such a way as to give the effect of a sleeve. A great many of the tunics for women were folded over at the neck line in the front and back to form a bib which hung down almost to the waist or in some instances even lower. The fullness of this part of the garment was laid in with a large box pleat in the center. In other tunics which are shown in Greek sculpture and vase painting, the garments appeared to be made of material which was accordion or side pleated. The men's tunics do not show this kind of pleating except in rare instances.

The cloak, which at times formed the entire costume of a man, was worn in a great variety of ways. The cloak worn by figure 1 in Plate 5 is a type of garment referred to. This may have been worn with one end dropping over the left shoulder as low as the ankle, the other end drawn across the back diagonally from the left shoulder under the right arm and again thrown over the left arm or left shoulder, leaving the neck and right arm and shoulder exposed. If the cloak should be worn as a costume in this way a short tunic similar to the one on Figure 3, but fastened only on the left shoulder, might be worn as an under garment.

53

In costuming Greek figures a very popular mistake is to show them dressed in white or pale pastel shades. This was not true in Greek life. The Greeks were fond of color; they polychromed their buildings; they even colored their statues to make them more life-like, and in their clothes they would certainly use color for which they showed a great fondness. The colors used were brilliant, such as terra cotta, yellow ocher, ultramarine blue, yellow, orange, green, purple and black. For example, a cloak or tunic might be of terra cotta red with a border of deep blue or black or diapered with leaves.

The sandals which were worn by the Greeks had soles of leather with thongs which laced over the instep around the ankle. In Greek tragedy a sandal with a very thick sole about two inches high was worn by the leading characters. In comedy the characters wore socks or a kind of buskin, which was cut like a moccasin and reached half way up the calf of the leg. This was allowed to fall down in folds around the ankle. Slaves were usually barefooted and in Greek dances it is also advisable for the dancers to wear no sandals.

Greek men and women of ordinary station wore the fillet. Other women wore their hair long, hanging down their backs, with one lock hanging in front, while still others of leading importance may have their hair coiffed with a knot high in the back and wearing a bandeau or coronet, or a veil wound tightly about the head, which gives slightly the effect of a turban.

Materials used in making these costumes should be linen, unbleached muslin, albatross or voile. Cotton flannel and ratine should be used for cloaks.

REFERENCES

Hottenroth, "Costume"
Hopes, "Costume of the Ancients"
Malliot, "Recherches sur les Costumes des Anciens Peuples"

SOME PLAYS AND CHARACTERS FOR WHICH GREEK COSTUMES ARE APPROPRIATE

Gods and Goddesses of Greek Mythology
  Zeus
  Hera
  Venus
  Artemis
  Hermes, etc.

Æsthetic and Interpretive Dances

Fairies

Symbolical Characters:
  Agriculture
  Truth
  Loyalty, etc.

Trojan Heroes
  Paris
  Hector
  Helen of Troy
  Achilles
  Antigone, etc.

Midsummer Night's Dream

Troilus and Cressida

Winter's Tale

Tennyson's Princess

Pygmalion and Galatea

55

PLATE V

No. 1 shows a costume which may be used for a king or a national hero. He is wearing a tunic which is cut straight, fastened over the shoulders and showing the typical cloak draped over the arms. The tunic could be of black and green with a cloak of terra cotta red, edged with a black stripe and patterned with small black circles or dots.

No. 2 shows a costume which may be worn by a shepherd or a peasant. He wears a round hat of felt or straw, a simple tunic, very short, and a short cloak.

No. 3 is the figure of a youth or an athlete wearing a very simple short tunic which is shorter at the sides than the front and back and is girdled in at the waist. He is also wearing the fillet and sandals. It will be noted that his hair is short and is combed forward over his forehead to form bangs.

No. 4 shows a type of soldier with armor. The corselet and shoulder plates are made of scale armor under which is worn a short pleated tunic. With this costume and also No. 3 short trunks are worn. The helmet is typical in form and the feathers around the crown should be red ostrich or some material such as yarn or silk thread which would give the effect of feathers. The armor can be executed in metal and metallic oilcloth by cutting the oilcloth in strips which are scalloped on one edge and stitched to a lining made of heavy domestic and fitted to the figure. The shield which is decorated with an octopus and outlined with a wide band could be made of beaver board or some similar material and painted in two strongly contrasting colors.

Fig. 1   Fig. 2   Fig. 3   Fig. 4

With the Greeks as well as many nations of that time and later the longer tunics denoted the dignity of kings as in figure 1. The youth of figure 3 is freer and simpler as is the peasant of figure 2 with his hat and coat. The soldier of figure 4 wears the same tunic only pleated and cut in points under his armor.

57

PLATE VI

No. 1 is the costume of a woman wearing a cloak draped in stiff folds over a tunic with a bib, the border of which can be seen between the cloak's folds. The lower part of the tunic is patterned with dots and crosses. This could be executed effectively in black for the cloak, deep orange for the tunic edged at the neck, the bib and the hem, and patterned with white or light yellow.

No. 2 a simple tunic of soft material to fall in many folds, is made with bibs, back and front, and is tied round the waist and drawn up to blouse over the hips.

No. 3 shows the figure with a tunic and super-tunic fastened over the right shoulder. A band will have to be placed under the bib so that the folds can be stitched in and remain in place. The bib and the hem are edged with a wide border of simple but effective design. The sleeves are formed by drawing the tunic up under the arms so as to fall in folds. The long shoulder seam or arm seam which reaches from the shoulder to the bend of the arm is caught together at intervals of about two and a half inches by round buttons or ornaments leaving an open space in between. The hair is dressed with a knot at the back and is wound in a veil.

No. 4 shows the Doric tunic, which was made perfectly straight, seamed on the edges on the left side and on the right side seamed in from the edge of the front and back about six or eight inches, and a bib, cut in a narrow panel as wide as the neck opening, was left to fall down almost to the waist. The garment was fastened on the shoulders by drawing the back part over the front and caught with a brooch or pin.

Fig. 1   Fig. 2   Fig. 3   Fig. 4

The elaborate folds of figure 1 were used by the queens and noble women of early Greece. Figure 2 is the costume worn by the lower class women, figures 3 and 4 are of later date.

ROMAN COSTUMES

The Roman costume was composed chiefly of two garments, a cloak and a tunic. The tunics worn by the men were either long or short according to the station of the person wearing them. Men of the upper classes, senators, etc., wore the long tunic; also boys of the same classes wore long tunics which came slightly above their ankles. Over this was worn the toga. Boys of all classes wore the bulla, which was a talisman hung around the neck on a cord or strap. Upper-class boys wore gold medallions of about two and a half or three inches in diameter. Boys of the lower classes had them made of leather. The toga which was cut circular on one side and the other edge rounded slightly and folded over, was worn over the left shoulder so the end reached the ground, then passed diagonally across the back under the right arm and again over the left arm, leaving the right arm free. The side which was first passed over the left shoulder was then drawn up in front to form a kind of pocket. The tunic was always fastened in at the waist with a girdle or cord. Sandals of leather with leather soles and fastened with leather thongs were worn by all classes. Women wore the tunic and super-tunic and a long scarf or veil which was worn over the head and wound around the body. There was also a sort of cloak or circular cape with a hood which was worn by the Romans and is used still in parts of Italy and other parts of Europe which were reached by Roman influence. This garment was fastened at the neck where the hood was sewed on and opened down the front.

The frescoes and paintings of the Romans show garments of great variety of colors. Greens, yellows, reds, browns of every shade, and many shades of blue and yellow were worn by all classes. White carried with it a mark of distinction and purple was reserved for the ruling classes. The materials which were used in the early Roman period were linen and wool. It was not until about the fourth century A. D. that silk came into popularity. In fact, it was not until the reign of Heliogabalus that this material became popular.

The tunics worn by Roman women were chiefly one type, the straight tunic with the long shoulders. This gained its variety of line through the girdling which had several variations. The stola or scarf which was worn may have been like a thin cashmere shawl or of a very fine material which was more like a veil than a shawl. This was draped around the body and over the shoulders in a great variety of lines and was very often worn over the head. This type of tunic is adapted for use in symbolic and æsthetic dancing.

The materials which can be used in making these garments are challis, linen, silk crêpe, or in cheaper materials, cotton crêpe, voile, cotton flannel, unbleached muslin and lawn.

BIBLIOGRAPHY

Metropolitan Museum Catalogue of Roman Sculpture
Racinet, "Le Costume"
Hottenroth, "Costume"
Hopes, "Costume of the Ancients"   .
Malliot, "Recherches sur les Costumes des Anciens Peuples"
Encyclopædia Britannica, "Costume"

SOME CHARACTERS AND PLAYS FOR WHICH THESE COSTUMES ARE APPROPRIATE

Gods and Goddesses of Roman Mythology
  Aphrodite
  Jupiter
  Diana
  Juno
  Mercury, etc.

Coriolanus
Anthony and Cleopatra
Julius Cæsar

Symbolic Characters
  Goddess of Liberty
  Justice   .
  Eternity, etc.

Nero
Ben Hur
Heralds

PLATE VII

No. 1. Man wearing a tunic of a type worn by lower classes fastened on the left shoulder and girdled in at the waist. Sandals may or may not be worn with this costume.

No. 2. Soldier wearing a helmet, corselet, tunic with short trousers and sandals. The corselet and shoulder pieces can be made of strips of belting stitched together and painted with metallic paint. The helmet can be made of a felt cap cut and shaped so the front, when turned up, will give the effect shown in this design. The side pieces are attached to this cap and fastened under the chin. This also should be painted with metal paint. The shield is the octagonal shape which was used by the Romans instead of the round shield which the Greeks used.

No. 3 shows the tunic and toga worn by the Romans.

No. 4 shows the cloak and tunic of an emperor. The cloak should be made of red or purple and banded with a gold border, and the tunic is of soft white material. The sleeves of the tunic are not shaped but are formed by allowing the tunic to be very wide and tying it in at the waist, the upper part then falls down over the arm.

Fig. 1   Fig. 2   Fig. 3   Fig. 4

As in the Greek, we find the social grades of the Romans. Figure 1 is the peasant, figure 2 the warrior, figure 3 the nobleman or senator, and figure 4 the king.

PLATE VIII

No. 1 shows a woman wearing a simple tunic girdled above the waist line with a circular cloak fastened on the right shoulder and cut shorter in the front than the back. Her hair is dressed in rolls of short tight curls.

No. 2 shows a woman wearing a long scarf over her head and left shoulder, under the right arm and thrown again over the left arm. Her hair is dressed low over the forehead in curls with a coronet.

No. 3 shows the tunic with a long shoulder seam caught together in three places and a tunic girdled with ribbons both above and below the waist line. This tunic is made very long, and after it is put on, a ribbon about two inches wide is drawn under the bust, under the arms, crossed in the back, the ends passing upward over the shoulders and drawn under the arms again and tied in the back. Then the fullness which forms the sleeves is drawn up at the side and the folds drawn up and arranged in front over the breast. Another ribbon is tied over the hips, fastened in front, and the folds which blouse over the hips are drawn up so that the edge of the tunic barely reaches the floor.

No. 4 shows a woman with an over-tunic girdled high and an under-tunic of different material. The over-tunic is of one color and the under-tunic of white. The Roman head band is used on the hair, which is drawn to a knot by coiling a braid on the crown of the head. The over-tunic of this dress may be worn without the underdress and cut to the knees. Such a tunic may be used for æsthetic dancers.

Fig. 1   Fig. 2   Fig. 3   Fig. 4

Figure 1 is the costume of the slave or lower class woman. Figure 2 strangely enough is the dress worn by Roman courtesan and empress alike. Figures 3 and 4 represent the wealthy class and the nobility.

MEDIÆVAL COSTUME

This period shows a marked change in the costume, for it was at this time that the fitted garment began to develop—that is, garments were cut to conform to the human figure. Although this did not develop to any great degree until somewhat later, it was at this time that the change took place. The tunics which formerly had been merely straight garments with a variety of folds were now developed into form-fitting or semi-fitting garments. Sleeves which were used very little in earlier periods now became the common order. Leg coverings such as tights and a sort of trousers made of tubes drawn over the legs and fastened at the waist and around the ankles were commonly used. As civilization moved northward it became necessary to adopt certain elements in clothes which were protective. Tunics were still worn by both men and women, but these were invariably made with sleeves. The sleeve, which was for the most part simply a straight tube, was either scant or full. Sleeves were also made much longer than the arms, so they could be turned down and keep the hands warm. When these sleeves were folded up over the wrists the folds formed a cuff. Cloaks which had formerly been quite simple in construction were now circular and fitted over the shoulders. The most common type was fastened across the front with a band or cord with ornaments on either side where the fastening was attached. The colors which were used were quite brilliant, such as brilliant blues, greens, vermilions, yellows of pure intensity. With these were also used a great variety of browns, many shades of gray, black and white. The wimple which was worn so much and is always associated with this period was probably used because of the added warmth which it gave. The wimple was a band of linen which was fastened on the top of the head and under the chin covering the sides of the face and the chin. It was also used to cover the neck. Cowls which were an added protection were very commonly used and were made with a short circular cape-like part which covered the shoulders. They were not commonly attached to the garment proper but were put on like a sort of cap. Buskins and shoes with slightly pointed toes became common in the 12th and 13th centuries. Even people of the lower classes in many instances were able to wear these. Lower-class men were usually dressed in a short tunic reaching about to the knees and with a tight leg covering like a tube, and buskins. The tunic was tied in at the waist. Women wore long dresses and underdresses, some of them semi-fitted over the upper part of the body. Women's sleeves for the most part were narrow. In some instances women wore a garment with long sleeves and over this a sort of tunic of the same color with short shoulder seams, large armholes and round neck. These over-garments in most instances were six or eight inches shorter than the under-garment which reached to the ground.

Children's costumes were similar to those of grown people, except they were usually shorter. Veils were worn over the head and were very often short, just reaching below the shoulders in the back. The hoods which were worn by women were usually rounded instead of being pointed at the back like the men's. Borders of plain colors and wide bands and stripes around the skirts were used a great deal.

It was at this period that brocades began to come into Europe from the East and people of wealth and the nobility wore materials of rich color and design. Embroidery was also employed. Fur was used for trimming and lining cloaks. Materials for making these costumes can be dyed muslin, colored and stenciled sateens to imitate silks, cotton crêpe, ratine in colors and a thin grade of turkish toweling dyed any desired color. Cretonnes may also be used. The chain armor can be made of a coarse knitted material and painted with silver paint. An ordinary knitted helmet such as the ones used in the army in the World War could be used for a chain helmet.

REFERENCES

Hottenroth, "Le Costume"

A. Von Heiden, "Trachtenkunde"

Planche, "Cyclopedia of Costumes"

I. H. Von Hefner-Altneck, "Trachten Kunstwerke"

"Les Arts Sumptuaires"

Racinet

SOME CHARACTERS AND PLAYS FOR WHICH THESE COSTUMES MAY BE USED

King Arthur

Launcelot

Guinevere

All's Well That Ends Well

As You Like It

Macbeth

Twelfth Night

Comedy of Errors

Hamlet

Ivanhoe

Richard I

Pied Piper

Merchant of Venice

Romeo and Juliet

Crusaders

Heralds

PLATE IX

No. 1 shows the figure of a boy wearing a short tunic with long sleeves turned up to form cuffs. The tunic is girded at the waist. On his legs he is wearing tights and a pair of soft buskins turned down to form a cuff. In this figure can be seen the type of hood with a point hanging down the back which was worn a great deal by men. Instead of the elongated point the hood can also be made with a short point, at the back, which stands out. These hoods should be made to fit snugly over the head as the people who wore them had them fitted to suit their size. This costume could be used by a page or a herald and without the hood might be worn by peasants and boys of lower classes.

No. 2 is a costume of a man of better class and consists of a long tunic, a cloak and shoes. Under the tunic are worn tights and a short tight-fitting garment with tight sleeves which would be worn indoors by the same man without cloak and long tunic. The cloak and tunic should be of contrasting colors.

No. 3 shows a knight in chain armor with a helmet also made of chain. Over this he is wearing a sleeveless tunic slashed over the left leg and girdled around the waist. This tunic was made of some brilliant colored material such as red with gold crosses or blue with gold crosses and similar tunics of striped material, the stripes being about three inches wide and of alternating colors, were also worn.

No. 4 shows the figure of a king wearing a cloak probably of silk material with a brocaded pattern banded with embroidery and faced with a plain material of another color. Under this he wears a tunic of rich material banded at the bottom with a broad band of design and also at the edge of the sleeves which are shorter than those of the under-garment. This tunic is slashed at the bottom and shows tights underneath, and a facing of some other material. He is wearing the pointed shoes which are characteristic.

Fig. 1   Fig. 2   Fig. 3   Fig. 4

The Middle Ages brought marked changes. Figure 1 is a peasant boy with his short tunic and cowl. Figure 2 a man of the upper class; the color, material and decorations denoting a prince or knight. Figure 3 is a warrior, an excellent design for a Crusader. The costume for a king of the period is shown in figure 4.

PLATE X

No. 1 is a woman wearing a long-sleeved dress with a super-tunic of the same color with bands of another color. Her head is wrapped in linen with a wimple drawn under the chin.

No. 2 shows the figure wearing a circular cloak cut short in front to allow freedom for the hands. This is put on over the head and fastened up at the neck. Around her shoulders is seen the lower part of a gorget with the hood pushed back. It is the same as the hood worn by Figure 3. The dress is in two parts with a super-tunic shorter than the undergarment.

No. 3 shows the long-sleeved semi-fitted type of garment which developed at this time. The skirt was caught up in front and thrown over the arm, exposing an undergarment of different color.

No. 4 shows the costume of a queen with crown, veil, cloak and dress of a design characteristic of the period. The cloak is made of a rich figured material and a border of embroidery. The facing is of a plain material of another color or might be a fur lining. It is fastened together across the front with a silk or gold cord looped over or buttoned. The dress is slightly fitted and has rather full tapering sleeves which are short, showing an undergarment of some soft material which covers the wrist. The sleeve and edge of the skirt are banded with embroidery and jeweled. The long braids which hang down have colored ribbons woven into them, the ends of which are used to tie the braid.

Fig. 1   Fig. 2   Fig. 3   Fig. 4

The social grades of the women of the Middle Ages were also marked more by material and decorations than line. Figure 1 is a servant. Figure 2 is a middle class woman, a costume also good for many religious characters. Figure 3 is a noble lady and figure 4 is a queen, costumes also apropriate to use for a saint.

75

EARLY RENAISSANCE 15TH CENTURY

The costume of the early Renaissance retains some of the characteristics of mediæval dress at the same time other features were developing. The fitted garment became more tightly fitted and was made in two parts, the bodice and the skirt. However, the skirt was still attached. Sleeves which had formerly required very little shaping now became more varied. They were either very closely fitted or full and flowing. Bandings of furs were used and many rich damasks, brocades and embroidered materials became very popular. Headdresses which had formerly been quite simple now became very elaborate and varied. The steeple headdress, the hennin and horn headdresses are always associated with this period.

A great many colors were used at this time and were usually of a richer hue than in the period preceding. Deep blues, maroon, greens, purples, browns of every shade and almost every other color was used, but always in rich combinations. The designs and the fabrics were usually carried out in two or three colors and were very bold. These patterns are particularly effective in stage costumes. Combinations of orange and yellow, red and black, green, yellow and blue, orange and green, or simple black and white are some of the color schemes which might be used.

It was at this time also that the scalloped edges were worn. These scallops in some costumes were so numerous that every edge was ornamented this way.

The neck line also changed and became wider over the shoulders. The neck line which formerly had been round and quite high was now cut square or pointed in front and widened over the shoulders. This was usually edged with fur, braid or an embroidered border. The skirts were very wide at the bottom and came to the ground. In the dress of lower-class women the skirt is often shown tucked in at the waist and showing the petticoat underneath.

The sleeves of outer garments were often lengthened so as to reach almost to the ground, and were slashed to the elbow or above, permitting the sleeve of an undergarment to show. The facing of these slash sleeves was of a different material from the outer part.

The shoes of this period were similar to the ones previously worn, but became more elongated and pointed. The toes were stuffed in order to keep the shape.

Men wore tights or hose which were often of two or three colors. Sometimes with one leg of one color and the other another color, or the leg was divided into two colors. The color is divided in points just below the knee.

BIBLIOGRAPHY

"Zur Geschichte der Costume"
Hottenroth, "Les Costumes"
Violette-le-duc, Dictionnaire Raissonne, V, vols. 3 and 4
Boutel de Wounel, "Jeanne d'Arc"
Shaw, "Dresses and Decorations of the Middle Ages"
Racinet, "Les Costumes Historiques"
I. H. Von Hefner-Altneck, "Trachten Kunstwerke"
Rhead, "Chats on Costume"

Meiuling   Van Eyck

SOME PLAYS AND CHARACTERS FOR WHICH THESE COSTUMES ARE USED

Merry Wives of Windsor   Fairy Tales (not Folk Tales)
                                              Cinderella
Henry VIII   Bluebeard, etc.

Measure for Measure   Pages

The Tempest   Jesters

Two Gentlemen of Verona   Playing cards—Early Tudor

Joan of Arc   Columbus

Frances I   Isabella

Charles the Great   Faust

Lorenzo de Medici   Mephistopheles

Lucretia Borgia   Robin Hood

                                            Heralds with tabards

                                            Gnomes

PLATE XI

No. 1. Man wearing cap with elongated top like a stocking cap, a cloak or coat with scalloped sleeves, hose and pointed shoes. This is an ordinary lower-class type of garment and may be worn with or without the long straight piece known as the tabard which hangs down the back and front.

No. 2 is a costume which could be worn by a page, herald or young man with or without the cap. The doublet can be made of a brocade with slashed sleeves as it is shown, or with close sleeves or sleeveless and showing the sleeves of the undergarment. For boys of lower classes this garment should be made of plain colored material. If it is worn sleeveless it should hang loose and the girdle be worn underneath.

No. 3 shows a young man wearing a loose-fitting coat with wide sleeves with a doublet underneath, cut very low and pointed in front and laced across with a shirt underneath. The hose show the manner in which they were often made of two or three colors. He is wearing a chain with a pendant and a round, flat cap.

No. 4 is a costume which was worn a little later and shows variety of slashing on the sleeves and over the chest, which permitted the lining or undergarment to show. The trousers are very full and made of strips of figured material and lined with a material of another color.

Fig. 1   Fig. 2   Fig. 3   Fig. 4

The Early Renaissance begins to lose the simplicity of line of earlier times. Figure 1 is that of a lawyer, a rich merchant, an older and dignified man. Figure 2 is the page or youth. Figure 3 a nobleman, a prince; the same lines in richer material are used by the kings. Figure 4 is the dress of the middle class man, the tradesman.

PLATE XII

No. 1. A woman with a headdress of starched linen folded and fastened under the chin and a white veil hanging down her back. The veil may be eliminated. The dress is a simple fitted garment with long tight sleeves, high waist line, and skirt caught up in front and fastened in at the waist, exposing an underskirt with a band of colored material.

No. 2 shows the figure of a queen with a crown worn over a cap of velvet and a mesh of gold or silk thread at the back. This same mesh is used to fill in the neck, which is cut square. The dress is made of heavy brocaded material and very full in the skirt. Around her neck she is wearing two necklaces, one a heavy chain with a pendant, the other a short string of jewels.

No. 3 shows the figure with a cloak falling from the shoulders and a dress which is fitted, and banded with fur.

No. 4 shows the steeple headdress with a veil, which was sometimes draped over the arm or left to flow free behind. The dress is fitted and has a wide fur collar.

Fig. 1   Fig. 2   Fig. 3   Fig. 4

As with the costumes of the men of the Early Renaissance so those of the women begin to lose simplicity of line. Figure 1 is a serving woman, figure 2 a queen, figure 3 a noblewoman who has only to change her headdress for a crown to make her also a queen. Figure 4 is a woman of the middle class whose gown simplified is appropriate to be worn by a woman of the lower class. A change in brocade, color, jewelry and headdress makes a change of caste.

PLATE XII-A

No. 1 is a Robin Hood costume with doublet and hose of green or brown material, pointed high shoes and a belt.

No. 2 is a costume to be used for heralds or pages. Over the doublet, which has a plain round collar and tight sleeves with turn-back cuffs, is worn a tabard which may be of a plain color or parti-colored.

No. 3 is a jester with tight cap with gorget, a short tunic with tight sleeves, and a belt. The sleeves are cut into points at the wrist and below the waist. Bells are sewed to the points.

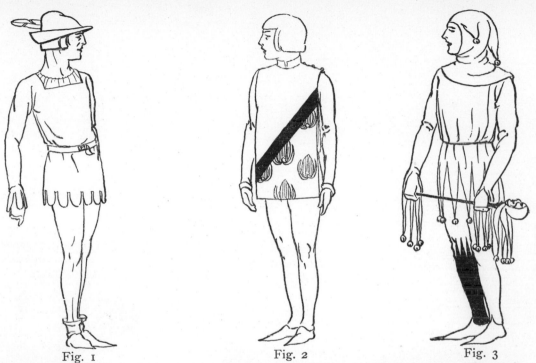

Fig. 1   Fig. 2   Fig. 3

This plate is very interesting as it shows simple changes in a basic pattern. The tunic, belted and scalloped as in figure 1 for Robin Hood and without the scallops for a man of the lower class; straight and decorated as in figure 2 the same tunic dresses a page or herald; cut with long points, with bells and cowl added, it is good for the jester or fool.

LATE RENAISSANCE 16TH CENTURY

The 16th century brought with it many developments in art which affected the dress of the period. It was at this time that the rich materials, jewels and laces became extremely popular. Before this, lace was not worn and it now became the rage. Lace ruffles, collars, cuffs and edgings on caps which replaced the large headdresses of the preceding period were exceedingly popular. The bodice which had become tight fitting previously was now made with stays and the long stiff stomacher which extended below the waist line made its appearance. The skirts which were usually worn to the ground and were full had their fullness further exaggerated by hoops, or the vertugal, as it was called. This was the first time hoops were worn. From that time down to the present at intervals this type of skirt has made its appearance in hoops and crinolines.

The costumes of this period have been recorded with great accuracy by the painters of the period. The costumes of the early part of the century have been faithfully recorded for us by Holbein and Dürer. Men's clothes were also made of very rich materials and during the early part of the century were quite full. The trousers were full and came almost to the knees. They were sometimes slashed and lined with material of the same color. The coats which were short, reaching only about to the knees or a little above, were quite full with very full sleeves slashed on the outside and showing an under-sleeve also very full. Under the coat was worn a doublet and over this was worn a narrow belt. Shirts with narrow ruffles around the neck and down the front were worn. Jewelry was very popular, and in the portraits of the period are shown many men wearing gold chains around their necks, gold band rings and even small gold buttons and ornaments on their clothes and hats.

Toward the latter part of the century the trousers became much shorter and were nothing more than trunks which were slashed to show the lining and stuffed to make them stand out full. The coats shrank into tight-fitting jackets with tight sleeves. Ruffles of linen were worn on the collars and cuffs. Over the jacket was worn a short cape which was often worn only on one shoulder. Hats became smaller but still retained their plumes and trimmings.

The hose which were worn with the full trousers became long tights, and shoes, instead of being so broad and slashed at the toes, were more normal in shape.

Men wore their hair short and women wore wigs which they changed and very often changed the color with the wig. The hair was dressed quite simply and jewels were worn in it. Small caps of linen and lace with a peak over the forehead were worn.

It is important to choose substitutes carefully, when selecting materials for the costumes of the late Renaissance period; the illusion of richness and a lavish use of decoration must be given.

Cretonnes with large elaborate designs picked out by embroidery, make fine substitutes for brocades. A more colorful way of simulating brocades is that of stenciling designs on material with a generous use of gold and silver as well as colored paint. Wooden button-molds painted or gilded may be used as substitutes for the enamelled and jeweled buttons of the period. Good inexpensive materials for these costumes are: sateens, cotton velvets, all mercerized cotton goods, and some qualities of silk eponge. In order to get the effect of rigidity necessary in bodices of this period, buckram must be used with a lavish hand. The vital thing in carrying out the dress of the women of this period is the silhouette, which must be not only correct as to its pinched waist-line and bouffant hips, but must give the effect of an almost steel-like stiffness.

BIBLIOGRAPHY

"Zur Geschichte der Costume"
Hottenroth, "Le Costume"
Racinet, "Historie du Costume"
Planchet, "Cyclopedia of Costume"
Jacquemin, "Iconographic du Costume"
Rhead, "Chats on Costume"

Quennell, "A History of Everyday Things in England"
Holbein
Duree
Portraits

SOME CHARACTERS AND PLAYS FOR WHICH THESE COSTUMES MAY BE USED

Catherine di Medici
Much Ado About Nothing
Taming of the Shrew
Othello
Elizabeth
Huguenots

Marie Stuart
Love's Labor Lost
James I
Richelieu
Charles I

PLATE XIII

No. 1 shows a man wearing the flat plumed hat of the early part of the 16th century. The outer coat with slashed sleeves and the short full trousers are made of velvet or some heavy silk. Long stockings and very broad shoes are characteristic of this period.

No. 2 is a boy or young man wearing a cap which hangs down at the side of the face, a short cape, tight-fitting blouse with slashed and puffed sleeves, tights and broad-toed shoes. The shirt has a band at the neck and is edged, and, for the first time, a frill is seen at the wrist.

No. 4 shows a small hat, tight short blouse with ruching at the neck and wrists, and very full short trunks and tights. Note the necklace which is typical of the period and is worn very wide over the shoulders instead of close to the neck. These were worn by both men and women. With this costume was also worn a short cape like No. 2, but of very rich brocade edged with gold or silk braid.

Fig. 1   Fig. 2   Fig. 3   Fig. 4

The Late Renaissance brought more changes. Here again the difference of material and decoration makes social distinctions. Figure 1 shows a nobleman's costume which by elaboration becomes the costume of the king. Figure 2 is the costume worn by a page or by a man of the populace. Figure 3 is the simple costume of the upper class. Figure 4 the young nobleman.

PLATE XIV

No. 1 is the costume of a young woman of the lower classes showing the plain linen cap, tight bodice with square neck and a full skirt. Over the skirt is worn a full narrow apron. The shoes with high tops which fall down around the ankle are the type worn by the lower classes.

No. 2 shows a costume with a small cap or kerchief on the head, one point coming over the forehead, a dress with full sleeves, wide cuffs and tight bodice cut square at the neck. The skirt is open in front to show a petticoat of another material. This could be of a striped or figured material, but not too elaborate, as this costume was worn by people of the middle classes.

No. 3 is more elaborate with a lace-edged cap, slashed sleeves, lace cuffs, fur facing on the skirt and an elaborately brocaded petticoat.

No. 4 is the type of gown worn by the court. The enormous lace collar is distinctive of the period, also the very tight bodice which was bound. The wide skirt was exaggerated by the hoops which came in at this period and were very wide over the hips.

Fig. 1   Fig. 2   Fig. 3   Fig. 4

The Late Renaissance brought the hoop skirt for women. Figure 1 is a servant or peasant, figure 2 a middle class woman, figure 3 as she stands is a noble lady, but with a change of headdress the costume is appropriate for Mary Stuart and other queens. Figure 4 is the more elaborate costume of Queen Elizabeth and the royal ladies of her time.

93

17TH CENTURY

The skirts of this period, although still very full, were not supported by a hoop. The overskirt was open in front and caught back to show the petticoat, which was of the same material or embroidered. Lace was worn a great deal but the high standing collar which was still worn in the early part of the century gradually became smaller and then developed into a wide collar which was turned back over the shoulders, which with the round neck line and short puffed sleeves gave the shoulders a sloping line. These collars fastened in front with a small bow of ribbon and were edged with lace. Lace cuffs with points were worn on the short sleeves and where the sleeves were puffed the puffs were caught together with small bows. The bodices were tight with a slight point in front. The materials which were used were usually plain. Feather fans were used and the hair was drawn back from the face and fastened in a knot at the back of the head. Ringlets hung down over the ears at the sides of the face and only the natural hair was worn.

Men's trousers were lengthened to the knees and were fastened to the coat by laces which were drawn through eyelets and tied in bows around the waist. The waist line was shortened and wide collars with lace edging were worn turned down over the shoulders during the early part of the century. They wore high boots with wide bell tops and square toes. Large buckles were worn on both shoes and boots. For an outer garment the cape was worn. These were very full and were also worn by women but usually with a hood attached. The hair was worn longer and pointed beards were the fashion. This was the age of the cavalier, the musketeer and the pirate.

Toward the end of the century the costumes for men changed. The doublet developed into a waist-coat and the outer coat, which has never been discarded down to the present time, developed. This coat was long, reaching to the knees and had three-quarter length sleeves with wide cuffs which were formed by turning back the full-length sleeve and showing a facing of brocade. The trousers which were covered by the waistcoat were tied at the knee by ribbons and had a lace ruffle which hung down below the knee over the calf of the leg. The shoes still had square toes and were tied with a bow of ribbon. It was at this time that the stock collar and jabot were first worn. Wigs now became popular with men and the hair was worn long and curled, and wide flat-brimmed hats were the vogue. Swords were always worn on the left side hung on a wide strap. Shirts with ruffled cuffs were worn. Cotton flannel, beach-cloth, cotton ratine and eponge, cotton duyveteen, can be used as substitutes for the plain, heavy materials of this period. It is also necessary to use cotton cordu-roy and velvet, sateens and even plush to give the effect of the luxurious apparel of this time. Broad-cloth is the best material for capes and breeches of the Puritan type, and brocaded velvets for the cavalier. Heavy unbleached muslin painted in rich designs embellished with gold or silver will give an excellent effect of brocades. For the ruffles used so universally, tarlatan, organdie and cheap cot-ton lace may be used. It is possible to make the wide, flat-brimmed hat of the period worn by puritans and pilgrims out of heavy buckram covered with sateen. Boots and sword-belts may be made of black enamel cloth. Cavalier boot-tops may be cut from enamel cloth with a wide cuff at the top and stitched up to slip over the shoe with a strap under the instep holding it in place. There is a new classifica-tion in this period owing to religious differences, so that persons of the wealthy class may appear in simple or luxurious costume, according to their religion.

BIBLIOGRAPHY

"Zur Geschichte der Costume"
Jacquemin, "Iconographic du Costume"
Quennell, " A History of Everyday Things in England"

PAINTERS

Rubens   Vermeer
Van Dyck   Terborch
Rembrandt

SOME PLAYS AND CHARACTERS FOR WHICH THESE COSTUMES MAY BE USED

Charles I   Puritans
Louis XIV   John Alden
James II   Priscilla
Henrietta Maria   Miles Standish, etc.
Cromwell
Moliere   Pirates

PLATE XV

No. 1 is a man of lower class with a white shirt with wide cuffs and collar, wide-brimmed hat, cape, square-toed shoes, knee-length trousers and a sash around his waist. To make a pirate of him give him boots and a pistol under his girdle.

No. 2 is a Puritan who wore very simple clothes which were the opposite of the prevailing mode, being very severe in every line.

No. 3 is a cavalier with plumed hat, wide collar edged with lace, lace cuffs and large cape. He wears the wide top boots with buckles and square toes.

No. 4 shows the type of clothes which men wore at the end of the century with the long waistcoat, coat with wide cuffs, lace on the edge of the trousers and the elaborate wig which became popular then.

Fig. 1   Fig. 2   Fig. 3   Fig. 4

The 17th Century was a period of decided contrasts ranging from the simple Cromwellian to the ornate Louis XIV. Figure 1 is the pioneer who is made into a pirate by adding high boots and a large hat or a bandanna. Figure 2 is the Puritan type of the time, figure 3 the Cavalier, figure 4 the courtier who easily becomes the king by added magnificence.

99

PLATE XVI

No. 1 is a servant with a cap, tight bodice and full skirt. The apron is tied under the peplum.

No. 2 is a Puritan woman wearing a straight-brimmed hat with high crown and a buckle on the band. Under her hat she is wearing a cap of linen which completely covers her hair. The dress is made with tight bodice pointed in front and a full skirt. The white collar, cuffs and apron are characteristic of this type of dress.

No. 3 shows the round neck line, lace collar, puffed sleeves fastened with ribbons, and the overskirt caught back to display an embroidered petticoat. The hair is dressed plain with ringlets at the sides.

No. 4 shows the full puffed sleeves, the pointed lace collar and cuffs, the bow of ribbon where the collar fastens and the feather fan, all of which are characteristic features of the period.

Plain colored taffeta or satin was used in making this type of costume.

Fig. 1   Fig. 2   Fig. 3   Fig. 4

The contrasts in the women of the 17th Century were not so marked as the men, although the materials and the fanciful details and the use of lace made them seem so. This can be seen here; figure 1 is a servant, figure 2 the Puritan woman, figure 3 the court lady and figure 4 the queen, who becomes very regal with rich material and laces.

18TH CENTURY

This was one of the most gracious of all the periods in costume. The costumes were made of very rich fabrics, satins, silks and brocades. Embroidery and laces and fine linen were employed. Tricorn hats were popular and wigs which had become popular sometime previously were an essential of the wardrobe. Cavaliers and courtiers each had several in their possession and it was the duty of their menservants to keep them in order. Ruffled shirts were worn as well as lace hats, also stocks and ties. Tight-fitting breeches made of satin and of a color harmonizing with the dominant color of the coat and waistcoat were worn. Light-colored or white stockings, preferably of silk, were in vogue. Shoes were favored but boots were worn for riding and traveling. Swords were usually part of the costume and sticks were carried. The skirts of the coats were stiffened to make them stand out.

Men used cosmetics, patches and perfumes. Even a man like Voltaire did not consider these things unworthy of consideration for he had on his dressing table boxes for rouge, powder and patches.

Early in the century the wide skirt returned to fashion and was worn throughout until the middle of the nineties. The hoops reached their widest proportion during the Louis XV period. Through this entire time the colors which were popular were light shades, often striped or brocaded with a flower design. Narrow ruffles were used a great deal for edgings at the neck lines, down the front of the bodice and down the edge of the overskirt and across the bottom of the underskirt. Deep ruffles of lace were worn on the edge of the sleeves, and for a flounce on the petticoat satins, taffetas and some brocades were used. Striped materials were very popular, the stripes being narrow, not more than a quarter to half an inch in width.

Toward the end of the century the coiffeur became very elaborate and the hair was piled on the head with puffs at the sides, and to add to the height, ribbons, plumes and garlands were worn. Flowers were much used as ornaments, and garlands were worn across the bodice from the shoulder to the waist line on the opposite side. The bodice was very tight. Fans were used a great deal and were made of lace, ivory, and tortoise, and they were painted in panels. They were only of medium size.

Shoes were of satin or kid and in colors to match the gown.

It is difficult to find substitute materials which will give the effect of richness and daintiness so typical of this period. There are certain mercerized organdies, silkolines and striped silks, which are inexpensive and give a very good illusion of better material. There is no very good substitute for taffeta which was so much in vogue in this century. If the costume is to be used at a great distance from the audience under very special lighting effects, a light weight cambric may be used. Cambrics come in many of the lighter shades fashionable in the eighteenth century. Mercerized poplins are also good for this period, and lend themselves to the bouffant style of dress better than sateen. It is advisable, however, to use expensive materials, because the brocaded satins and velvets and beautiful silks were an expression of the civilization of that day.

BIBLIOGRAPHY

"Zur Geschichte der Costume"
"Costumes des Femmes Française"
Jacquemin, "Iconographic des Costumes"

PAINTERS

Watteau	Gainsborough
Fragonard	Reynolds
Nattier	Reaburn
Lancret	Chardin
Boucher	Hogarth

SOME PLAYS AND CHARACTERS FOR WHICH THESE COSTUMES MAY BE USED

Louis XV
Marie Antoinette
Madame du Barry
George II
George III
Catherine the Great
Lafayette

Jacobites

American Colonial:
Washington
Franklin
Paul Revere
Nathan Hale, etc.

School for Scandal

The Rivals

She Stoops to Conquer

PLATE XVII

No. 1 is a man of the lower classes wearing a waistcoat, breeches, shirt and buckled shoes. The waistcoat for servants and similar characters should be made of plain material.

No. 2 is a young dandy of the period with tricorn hat, brocaded waistcoat and coat and breeches which button at the knee. The waistcoat is open at the sides up to the waist, and when a sword is worn it is fastened to a belt around the waist and hung at this vent on the left side. The cuffs, which turn back six or seven inches, are slashed on the underside and buttoned to the sleeve on top. The hair, which is dressed in rolls at the side, is caught at the back with a bow of ribbon.

No. 3 shows a similar costume made of plain material and is the type which was common in America at this period. Note also the buckled shoes.

No. 4 is a type of dress which came in at the close of the century. The Napoleon hat, short vest and cutaway coat are the chief characteristics of this costume. The buckles on the shoes have been replaced by bows.

Fig. 1   Fig. 2   Fig. 3   Fig. 4

The knee breeches and the straighter coat of the 18th Century are shown here. In figure 1 the servant, in figure 2 the Cavalier, who only needs a sword to make the costume appropriate for Louis XV. In figure 3 a man of the middle class and in figure 4 is a man of the Directoire, that period of changing silhouette from Louis to the beginning of the 19th Century.

PLATE XVIII

No. 1 is the costume worn by a maid or nurse. It consists of a cap, dress with fitted bodice, full skirts, an apron with bib and a fichu tucked under the bib.

No. 2 is a little girl of the period dressed in just the same manner as an older person.

No. 3 shows a costume with the full skirt and tight bodice with the pointed front. Over the skirt is worn an apron of the same material as the bodice. The small cap, which was very popular, was ruffled all around.

No. 4 is a dress which was worn for formal occasions and was usually made of a brocade of flowers and ribbons on a light background. Note the neck line and the ruffles. The hair was drawn back from the face and curls hung over the left shoulder. Medium-sized fans were used. This type of dress was worn in America for formal occasions. The shoes or slippers were square toed and made of satin.

No. 5 is of a more severe style which was made to conform with the dress worn by the men of the period. The bodice and overskirt were made of a darker material, usually taffeta and often striped. The underskirt was of lawn and sometimes figured.

Fig. 1   Fig. 2   Fig. 3   Fig. 4   Fig. 5

Even as late as the 18th Century children dressed like grown-ups as is seen in figure 2, which corresponds to both the servant of figure 1 and the middle class woman of figure 3. Figure 4 represents the noblewoman of the period and also the queen of Marie Antoinette's time. Figure 5 is the Directoire, that changing period between Louis and the 19th Century.

DIRECTOIRE AND EMPIRE

The clothes of the period which followed the downfall of the monarchy in France were quite different in character from the ones worn throughout the eighteenth century. The silks which had been so popular previously gave way to more substantial woolen goods. The knee-length breeches became long tight-fitting trousers which buttoned up, from the ankle, on the lower calf almost to the knee. The long vests of brocade or embroidered materials were changed for vests which had revers cut in a V in front and which came only to the waist line. At each side was worn a fob. These pairs of fobs were worn by both men and women. Over the vest was worn a double-breasted coat with a wide collar, sleeves which were either straight with narrow cuffs or were slightly fitted with no cuffs.

Pumps and short boots were the current footwear.

Hats now developed a new style, and the beaver with the straight or bell crown was worn. High linen collars and stock ties were worn exclusively.

The dress of the women which at first resembled the masculine mode for street wear became more classic in its lines. At this time there was a great revival of interest in classicism and the clothes were greatly affected by it. The waist line was raised and sleeves for the most part were eliminated except for the short puffed sleeve at the shoulder. Long scarves and shawls were worn and were sometimes made with fur or marabou edging. The shoes were almost invariably very low and without heels. They were very like ballet shoes and were very often red.

III

The materials which were favored for ordinary wear were chiefly thin cotton goods and very often entirely white or white with a small printed figure. For evening gowns and cloaks the materials used were usually satin and velvet embroidered in gold or silver with a pattern of stars or wreaths and flowers.

During the Empire the colors which were popular were very heavy and rich, such as scarlet, royal blue, mustard yellow and green. Long gloves which reached above the elbow were worn in the streets and for evening. The fans which were used were small and usually spangled and had sticks of ivory.

Dresses were generally round length and cleared the ground four or five inches, but some evening gowns had trains which fell from the shoulders and were quite long and of velvet, lined with satin.

Hats had many different varieties. There was the cap which was made of lawn, Swiss or some other cotton material and was very much like the boudoir cap or mob cap. The bonnet with the high crown was worn at this period. It had a peaked brim which came far over the face and was fastened by this under the chin. Most novel of all was the stiff beaver with its tailored lines and cockades, which was only worn with dresses with long sleeves. Men wore striped and flowered vests.

Their suits were of various light colors, buffs and blues being the favorites. Like the period just before this, the characteristic quality of the times was expressed in the richness and elaborate decorations of dress. All substitute materials used in costuming plays of the Directoires and Empire period must give an illusion of expensive attire.

BIBLIOGRAPHY

Jacquemin, "Iconographic des Costumes"
Livre, "Modes et Usages au Temps du Marie Antoinette"
"Zur Geschichte der Costume"

PAINTERS

Ingres   David

SOME CHARACTERS AND PLAYS FOR WHICH THESE COSTUMES MAY BE USED

Napoleon	Marie Louise
Josephine	French Republic
Mme. Recamier	Charlotte Corday
Louise of Prussia	Louis Napoleon
Frederick William III	Vanity Fair: Waterloo

PLATE XIX

No. 1 is wearing a double-breasted coat with slightly shaped sleeves, cut away in front with a straight line at the waist and displaying a striped vest beneath with the stripes running horizontally. The trousers button at the calf and are tight fitting. The pumps have straps over the insteps.

No. 2 is a similar costume, but the coat has a fuller skirt and has breeches instead of trousers. Note the way the brim of the hat turns down in the back.

No. 3 is wearing a low-crowned beaver hat and a coat with shawl collar. It is fastened with frogs and is not cut away in front. Top-coats were made in a sweater fashion and reached below the knees, sometimes to the ankles.

No. 4 is wearing a cutaway coat, tight trousers and short boots with colored tops. The tops were usually buff or brown.

Fig. 1   Fig. 2   Fig. 3   Fig. 4

During the Directoire and the Empire periods the upper and lower classes began to have the same silhouette. The differences in social standing were more in materials, simple or elaborate decorations, footgear, and headdress.

PLATE XX

These dresses show the characteristics of the period, high waist line, short puff sleeves and round length skirts which clear the ground.

No. 1. The chief characteristics of this costume are the cap with ties, the long scarf and the gloves which come above the elbow.

No. 2 wears a bonnet with ties, a ribbon around the waist and long tight sleeves. Note the slippers.

No. 3 has a beaver hat with cockades, a wide ruffled collar with ruching at the neck, a long scarf edged with a ruffle or fur and several rows of edging around the bottom of the skirt.

No. 4 shows the hair dressed with bands and plumes, a dress with embroidered border and a cloak with sleeves and a high collar.

Fig. 1   Fig. 2   Fig. 3   Fig. 4

With the women as with the men during the Directoire and the Empire periods, the social caste was designated more by elaboration than line. Satin, velvet, embroideries, plumes were much used by the upper classes.

MID-VICTORIAN AND CIVIL WAR

The dress following the first Empire gradually developed the tight bodice or basque, as it was called, the skirts became wider and the waist line was lowered. By 1830 the crinoline was back in style, an interval of about thirty-five years. This was the prevailing style down to the close of the sixties when the hoops were narrowed at the sides and gradually became bustles, which were worn in the back. The most beautiful dresses of the century were those worn during the period between eighteen forty-five and sixty-five. By that time the skirts had reached their greatest width and the waists had been drawn in just as narrow as was possible. The petticoats were made with whalebone, grapevine, or rattan hoop and many ruffles to hold the skirt out. A very good way to make one of these petticoats is to make a very wide circular skirt. Into this sew three bands of feather boning or rattan (rattan is preferable as it has great elasticity and will support the weight of the skirt better); the first row should be placed over the hips, the second half way between the hips and the knees, the third just below the knees. Over these sew three flounces of tarlatan, which are deep enough to overlap and keep the hoops from showing. For dresses of lightweight materials, a very full tarlatan petticoat with several fine ruffles is all that is needed.

Gloves were worn on every public occasion and were never removed in public. They were always white kid and short. Just above the gloves was worn a pair of gold bracelets often decorated with black enamel. These were always worn with the ball or party dress. Wreaths and flowers worn in the hair, and nosegays in metal holders were carried. Men wore beaver hats, stock ties and frock coats of black or dark colored material. The trousers were usually light gray, buff or tan.

Materials for the Civil War period must simulate the light, crisp muslins, the taffetas and grosgrain silks of the time. These materials were always decorated, sometimes with stripes and sometimes with flowers. The muslins often carried a colorful design of fruits or flowers, giving the effect of a hand-painted design. The silks were woven into brilliant stripes or dainty flower designs, and sometimes shot with contrasting color. Rosettes of ribbon and silk and tulle were used lavishly as decorations. Flounces, piping and little frills were typical. Petticoats were a vital part of my lady's wardrobe. She sometimes wore four or five, each one carrying ten or twelve yards of material stiffened with feather-bone and worn on top of the hoop. All this weight hung from the waist which was rigidly enclosed in heavy corsets. The silhouette of the dress was most important and should be carefully carried out in costume.

Men's trousers were cut in what was known as the peg-top style, carrying great fullness around the waist, tapering to the foot where a strap went under the instep to hold the trouser in place. Broadcloths or duyveteen or flannel are the best materials from which to make men's clothes of this period.

Stovepipe and beaver hats were styles for men, while women were charming in poke bonnets of quilted silk or leghorn straw tied under the chin, trimmed in ribbons and flowers, or tiny roll-brim straw hats perched low on the forehead. It was a period of narrow shoulders and small hats.

BIBLIOGRAPHY

"Zur Geschichte der Costume"
Jacquemin, "Iconographic der Costume"
Uzanne, "Fashions in Paris"
"Godey's Lady's Book"

PAINTERS

Sully   Alfred Stevens

SOME PLAYS AND CHARACTERS FOR WHICH THESE COSTUMES MAY BE USED

Abraham Lincoln   American Pageants
Queen Victoria   Little Women
Napoleon III   Secret Service
Empress Eugénie   Barbara Frietchie
Disraeli

PLATE XXI

No. 1 is a man wearing a turn-over collar and stock tie, dark frock coat, double-breasted, and trousers with straps which fasten under the foot.

No. 2 wears a silk hat, turn-over collar, stock tie, cut-away coat, peg-top trousers with straps, and a brocaded vest. On a ribbon around his neck he is wearing a pince-nez, not a monocle.

No. 3 wears a standing collar, white stock tie and white shirt. The coat tails are cut several inches above the knees. The vest is of white, or embroidered and brocaded. Cuffs should show below the coat-sleeves, which are set into short shoulder seams and taper slightly.

Fig. 1   Fig. 2   Fig. 3

The Mid Victorian period brought in the beginning of the conventional dress for men, especially the evening clothes. The differences in social standing are marked more by the manner of wearing them and the care, although the brocaded waistcoat was a distinction.

PLATE XXII

No. 1 is a street gown with tight bodice and wide skirt with crinoline. The bonnet is made of the same material as the dress. This dress was probably made of taffeta or satin with trimming of velvet. These materials can be approximated with sateen or cambric trimmed with cotton flannel dyed the same or a harmonizing color.

No. 2 is a ball dress of white with satin bodice and tarlatan skirt trimmed with flowers. Short gloves and a pair of gold bracelets were worn with this dress.

No. 3 is a party or bridal gown with bands of ruching and a flounced skirt. The round neck was always made on wedding gowns.

Fig. 1   Fig. 2   Fig. 3

The women of the Mid Victorian period dressed much alike regardless of social caste. They differ greatly in materials and details; such as gloves, shoes, jewelry, but not in silhouette. Figure 1 is a dress for the street, figure 2 a ball gown and figure 3 an elaborate housedress.

VII

COSTUMING A RELIGIOUS DRAMA

THE costuming of Biblical plays when not used in the Church service is considered from the same point of view as costuming any other plays. The period of the play is noted, then the influence, whether Egyptian or Assyrian or Roman, and the designs made accordingly. The best source for such designs is the collection of pictures of "Old Testament Costumes," by Tissot.

However when a Morality Play or a Miracle Play is to be costumed, the usual routine is not the correct way to go about it.

During the early centuries of the Christian Church certain colors and methods of dressing became associated with the New Testament characters, and the great painters of the period immortalized the types from which today we costume the Holy Virgin, our Saviour, the Apostles and the Saints.

The Miracle and Morality Plays came into being during the Middle Ages and were often used as part of the Church service of worship. It is customary therefore to costume all such plays in the medieval costume rather than the historic period of the time of Christ.

In England Miracle and Morality Plays were largely produced by Craft Guilds. There are still extant programs which show that certain properties and costumes were always used for certain characters by the Guilds. For instance, Herod always wore a helmet, a painted visor and an elaborate gown of blue satin. His helmet and falchion were decorated with silver, gold and green foil; he carried a scepter. Judas always had red hair and a beard. The Devil always wore black leather, a mask with ragged features, and always carried a club. The Marys always wore flowered crowns, the Angels gold skins and wings. This way of costuming may or may not be followed exactly. It is a purely conventional manner.

Certain colors were also symbolically attached to certain characters in the Story of Christ. Mary the Mother is always in blue of a deep vivid quality. The Magdalen is usually dressed in scarlet. Saint Joseph is in a simple dark robe and never wears a headdress. The Saints, when they are men, are shown also without a headdress. Women saints usually wore the wimple of the Middle Ages and the straight robes and semi-fitted sleeves of the same period. The Christ is always shown in white with a crown, if after the Crucifixion.

The painters of Italy and Germany and Holland who have painted the most famous Biblical pictures set aside the historic costume of the Hebrews for those more intelligent to western sympathies and all our ideas have been largely influenced by them. Tintoretto, for instance, did not hesitate to turn every Biblical episode into a picture of what the scene would look like if it had taken place under his own eyes.

Any Nativity Play to be given may be safely costumed from the Italian Masters, unless the play is definitely a Mediæval Miracle Play. Then the mediæval dress should be used. "Bethlehem Tableaux," by John K. C. Cheshire, gives a definite painting for each group in a Nativity Play. He suggests the grouping and coloring of Giotto's "Annunciation" or Ghirlandajo's or Angelico's. For the "Visitation of St. Elizabeth" Ghirlandajo's "The Meeting of Mary and Elizabeth" is a beautiful model. "The Shepherds in the Field" may be grouped and costumed from Murillo or Josefa de Ribera. "The

Adoration of the Shepherds at the Manger" can have no better model than Murillo's "Adoration" or Correggio's "Nativity." "The Presentation in the Temple" may be taken from Carpaccio's painting of that title. "The Adoration of the Magi" has been the favorite theme of many painters. Filippino Lippi, Paole Veronese, Tintoretto and Burne-Jones have all given us pictures from which this grouping may be taken. Millais' painting of the "Boy Jesus in the Carpenter Shop" is very beautiful, and for pictures of the tragedy of the crucifixion there are none better than the paintings of Leonardo da Vinci, or later Rubens.

The most useful books for pictures and descriptions for Religious Plays are "The Gospels in Art," edited by W. Shaw Sparrow, published by Hodder and Stoughton, London, and "The Life of Christ as Represented in Art," by Dean Farrar. Other references are "The Primer of Production," from the Department of Religious Education of the Episcopal Church of America, 381 Fourth Avenue, New York City.

PLATE OF COSTUMES FOR RELIGIOUS DRAMA

No. 1, the Guardian Angel, wears a fillet of gold stars, gold belt, loin cloth of gold and mantle of gold. The loin cloth is cut slightly circular and folded across the front. The cloak is a straight piece of material which hangs loose in the back, is secured at one end under the belt in front, and is thrown over the left shoulder.

No. 2, the Devil's costume, is black with red quills on the cap, and red facing for the scalloped sleeves. The doublet and cape would be made of black jersey cloth. The hose are ordinary black tights.

No. 3 wears a dark cloak made straight with an opening down the front and a straight tunic with straight sleeves.

No. 4 wears a straight tunic tied with a cord at the waist. The sleeves are straight and turned back at the wrist.

No. 5 wears a straight tunic and a cloak which is rectangular, about 5 by 6 feet. To drape this cloak, first tie a cord about the waist, then place the long side of the cloak over the left shoulder and tuck the corner which hangs in front under the belt. Then take the other end, pass it diagonally across the back from the left shoulder to the right hip and pull the other corner through under the belt, thus securing the cloak.

Sandals are worn with all these costumes.

Domestic cotton flannel or thin turkish toweling should be used for the tunics. For the cloaks turkish toweling, cotton flannel or ratine of some color should be used.

Fig. 1 Fig. 2 Fig. 3 Fig. 4 Fig. 5

Figure 1. The guardian or militant angel. Figure 2 can be used for Lucifer, the devil or Mephistopheles. Figures 3, 4 and 5 are purely historic Biblical costumes, figure 4 being very good for the early Christian martyr or the figure of Christ.

PLATE OF COSTUMES FOR RELIGIOUS DRAMA

No. 1 wears a white veil which is made of a large square of material, a cloak which is straight with an opening six inches wide down the front, and a straight tunic girdled at the waist, with wide sleeves turned back at the wrist.

No. 2 is a costume of the Virgin Mary with a crown worn over a white or gray veil, a blue cloak edged with gold, and lined with gold over a tunic of white or gray.

No. 3 wears a long veil which is tied at the back of the head and a straight sleeveless tunic tied at the waist with a cord.

No. 4 is an angel wearing a tunic, which is fitted over the shoulders and bust and cut circular at the bottom, and a gold halo; and carrying a gold palm branch.

All these costumes have sandals.

Fig. 1 Fig. 2 Fig. 3 Fig. 4

Figure 1 for the Virgin Mary sainted. Figure 2 for a saint. Figure 3 with or without **the** veil is good for groups. Figure 4 is the conventional angel to which wings may be added.